Company La

2012–2013

Routledge
Taylor & Francis Group

LONDON AND NEW YORK

Eighth edition published 2012
by Routledge
2 Park Square, Milton Park, Abingdon, Oxon OX14 4RN

Simultaneously published in the USA and Canada
by Routledge
711 Third Avenue, New York, NY 10017

Routledge is an imprint of the Taylor & Francis Group, an informa business

© 2012 Routledge

First edition published by Cavendish Publishing Limited 1997
Seventh edition published by Routledge 2010

British Library Cataloguing in Publication Data
A catalogue record for this book is available from the British Library

ISBN: 978-0-415-68330-2 (pbk)
ISBN: 978-0-203-27203-9 (ebk)

Typeset in Rotis
by RefineCatch Limited, Bungay, Suffolk

MIX
Paper from
responsible sources
FSC
www.fsc.org
FSC® C004839

Printed and bound in Great Britain by
TJ International Ltd, Padstow, Cornwall

Contents

Table of Cases

Table of Statutes

Table of Statutory Instruments

Table of European Legislation

Directives

How to use this book

Welcome to this new edition of Routledge Company Law Lawcards. In response to student feedback, we've added some new features to these new editions to give you all the support and preparation you need in order to face your law exams with confidence.

Inside this book you will find:

░ NEW tables of cases and statutes for ease of reference

▨ Revision Checklists

We've summarised the key topics you will need to know for your law exams and broken them down into a handy revision checklist. Check them out at the beginning of each chapter, then after you have the chapter down, revisit the checklist and tick each topic off as you gain knowledge and confidence.

1

Sources of law

Primary legislation: Acts of Parliament	▨
Secondary legislation	▨
Case law	▨
System of precedent	▨
Common law	▨
Equity	▨
EU law	▨
Human Rights Act 1998	▨

■ Key Cases

We've identified the key cases that are most likely to come up in exams. To help you to ensure that you can cite cases with ease, we've included a brief account of the case and judgment for a quick aide-memoire.

HENDY LENNOX v GRAHAME PUTTICK [1984]

Basic facts

Diesel engines were supplied, subject to a *Romalpa* clause, then fitted to generators. Each engine had a serial number. When the buyer became insolvent the seller sought to recover one engine. The Receiver argued that the process of fitting the engine to the generator passed property to the buyer. The court disagreed and allowed the seller to recover the still identifiable engine despite the fact that some hours of work would be required to disconnect it.

Relevance

If the property remains identifiable and is not irredeemably changed by the manufacturing process a *Romalpa* clause may be viable.

■ Companion Website

At the end of each chapter you will be prompted to visit the Routledge Lawcards companion website where you can test your understanding online with specially prepared multiple-choice questions, as well as revise the key terms with our online glossary.

You should now be confident that you would be able to tick all of the boxes on the checklist at the beginning of this chapter. To check your knowledge of Sources of law why not visit the companion website and take the Multiple Choice Question test. Check your understanding of the terms and vocabulary used in this chapter with the flashcard glossary.

▦ Exam Practice

Once you've acquired the basic knowledge, you'll want to put it to the test. The Routledge Questions and Answers provides examples of the kinds of questions that you will face in your exams, together with suggested answer plans and a fully-worked model answer. We've included one example free at the end of this book to help you put your technique and understanding into practice.

QUESTION 1

What are the main sources of law today?

Answer plan

This is, apparently, a very straightforward question, but the temptation is to ignore the European Community (EU) as a source of law and to over-emphasise custom as a source. The following structure does not make these mistakes:

▦ in the contemporary situation, it would not be improper to start with the EU as a source of UK law;

▦ then attention should be moved on to domestic sources of law: statute and common law;

▦ the increased use of delegated legislation should be emphasised;

▦ custom should be referred to, but its extremely limited operation must be emphasised.

ANSWER

European law

Since the UK joined the European Economic Community (EEC), now the EU, it has progressively but effectively passed the power to create laws which are operative in this country to the wider European institutions. The UK is now subject to Community law, not just as a direct consequence of the various treaties of accession passed by the UK Parliament, but increasingly, it is subject to the secondary legislation generated by the various institutions of the EU.

Incorporation

1

Judicial exceptions

Combating fraud

Agency

Groups of companies

Trust

Corporate killing

INTRODUCTION

In this chapter, the aim is to introduce key areas of company law. Much of the content may not be the subject of a specific examination question but this area is vital to an understanding of company law. Key issues, such as corporate personality, are dealt with in some detail. The law relating to companies was amended by the Companies Act (CA) 2006. This Act both consolidates and reforms company legislation.

ORGANISING FOR BUSINESS

When a business person decides to set up in business, there are a variety of formats that can be adopted. These are sole trader, partnership or company. The decision as to which type of entity will be used will be influenced by a variety of factors, such as whether there are other people who will be involved in running the business, the size of the business, whether the business has any assets and how long the venture is likely to last. He or she will need to consider the various advantages and limitations of each form of organisation.

THE COMPANY AND THE PARTNERSHIP

The most usual initial decision is whether to operate as a partnership or as a company registered under the (CA) 2006. Reference here is to partnerships coming within the scope of either the Partnership Act 1890 or the Limited Partnerships Act 1907. Partnerships coming within the former can be referred to as ordinary or general partnerships. It is possible for a limited liability partnership to come into existence, as provided for by the Limited Liability Partnerships Act 2000. These types of partnerships are dealt with later on.

The two types of business are very different. A partnership is defined in s 1 Partnership Act 1890 as 'the relation which subsists between persons carrying on a business in common with a view of profit' (*Khan v Miah* [2000]). The company is a separate person in law (*Salomon v Salomon & Co Ltd* [1897]). The company can own property, commit crimes and conclude contracts. The partnership, on the other hand, is no more than a convenient term for describing the sum total of the partners who make up the partnership or firm. The partnership is not a separate person in law. The partnership cannot commit crimes or torts. These can only be committed by the partners, as agents of the firm.

A further consequence of the distinction between the company and the partnership is that the company pays corporation tax as a separate entity on its profits whilst the partnership does not pay tax as such, although a tax assessment may be raised against it. The tax is in fact paid under the schedular income tax system by the individual partners in the firm.

> ### ▶ SALOMON v SALOMON & CO LTD [1897]

Salomon incorporated his boot and shoe repair business. He took all the shares of the company except six which were held by his wife and children. Payment for the transfer of the business was partly by debentures (a secured loan) issued by the company to Salomon. The debentures were transferred to Broderip in exchange for a loan. Salomon defaulted on the loan and Broderip sought to enforce the security against the company. Unsecured creditors tried to put the company into liquidation. A dispute ensued as to who had priority in relation to payment of the debts. The unsecured creditors argued that Salomon's security was void as the company was a sham and was in reality the agent of Salomon.

The House of Lords held that this was not the case, the company had been properly incorporated and that therefore the security was valid and could be enforced.

The case is the most important case in company law since it is from this case that many of the principles of English company law flow. However, the spirit of the decision has not been universally followed and there are exceptions to the *Salomon* principle where the corporate veil is lifted.

ADVANTAGES OF INCORPORATION

The members of a registered company have the benefit of access to limited liability. Not all companies are limited. Indeed, there are many unlimited companies where liability of the members is not limited. The advantage of such companies is that they do not need to file annual accounts. By contrast, although there is such a thing as a limited partnership (see the Limited Partnership Act 1907), partnerships are in practice unable to limit the liability of the partners, unless it is a limited liability partnership created under the Limited Liability Partnerships Act 2000.

A feature of partnership is that partners are involved in the business either via the investment which they have made in the enterprise or by managing it. For a company however, we need to separate ownership from control. The people who subscribe for the shares of a company do not necessarily have any hand in the running of the business. This will be particularly true of a large public company. In the case of the partnership, all of the partners of the firm are agents and are able to act to bind the firm and are bound by the actions of the other partners.

Since the company is a separate entity, in theory, it could go on forever. Perpetual succession is seen as a benefit of incorporation as the company can continue even when those who run it or finance it may change. Partnerships, unless they have made arrangements in their partnership deed, have to be re-formed and reconstituted upon the death or bankruptcy of individual partners.

Where a person wishes to invest money and needs the investment to be readily realisable, the company is the appropriate vehicle. This is particularly true if the company is quoted on the Stock Exchange since there is a market mechanism for disposing of the shares of the business. In a partnership, it is likely that a partnership share will be much less easily realisable than shares in a company.

A further advantage for the company is in the context of raising finance. A company, as a separate entity, is able to mortgage all its assets by way of a floating charge to secure a borrowing from, for example, a bank. This means of securing a loan and raising finance is not available to the partnership.

The costs of incorporation are minimal. However, there are some formalities connected with setting up and running a company. The CA 2006 has stream-lined the paperwork required to set up a company. It is now possible to file the documentation online. Compliance with ss 7–16 of CA 2006 requires the filing of a modified form of the memorandum of association as well as an application for registration, articles of association and statements of initial shareholding, share capital, guarantee, proposed officers and statement of compliance. There are additional requirements regarding company management, the issuing of shares, the creation of charges and the filing of the annual return. Furthermore, the company is obliged to keep a series of company books at the company's registered office or some other appropriate place. These registers would include the register of members, register of directors and register of charges. However, a partnership does not even require a written agreement (Partnership at will). In this case it will be governed by the Partnership Act 1890 by default.

An important consideration for entrepreneurs who are setting up in business is what the tax consequences of setting up as a company or as a partnership will be. It is not possible to say that the balance of advantage always lies with one form of business rather than another, but it will certainly be a powerful consideration when entrepreneurs are weighing the relative advantages and disadvantages of each form of business medium. Partners will pay income tax on profits taken from the business; companies will pay corporation tax on profits made by the company; directors will pay income tax on salaries; and shareholders will pay tax on dividends received.

The information set out above in relation to different types of business is extremely important background information in tackling company law questions and understanding why people set up companies rather than operating a business through the medium of a partnership. The restriction on the number of partners forming a trading partnership was lifted in December 2002. Prior to that date the maximum number of partners that could be involved in a firm was set at 20.

PUBLIC COMPANIES AND PRIVATE COMPANIES

Another key area which permeates the whole of company law is the distinction between public companies and private companies. The vast majority of companies are private companies. Those that hit the news headlines tend, however, to be public companies and this may give a distorted view of the numerical significance of public companies.

The surprising feature of English company law is that the general principles apply to public companies as to private companies. However, the advent of CA 2006 has resulted in the removal 'of unnecessary [regulatory] burdens on small firms', with greater variation in the legal requirements placed on different types of companies.

A public company must have a minimum subscribed share capital of at least £50,000 or the Euro equivalent (s 763 of the CA 2006). This should be paid up to at least 25 per cent before it can be incorporated and commence its business (s 586 of the CA 2006). This was a requirement of the Second EC Directive which set the minimum subscribed share capital for public companies within the European Union. In addition to the payment of the minimum subscribed share capital to at least 25 per cent on initial allotment of shares, the whole of any premium must be paid up (for example, if a company issues 50,000 £1 par shares at £1.50, the minimum subscribed share capital would be £37,500, that is, one quarter of £50,000 plus premium of £25,000).

A further distinction between the public and private company is found in the company name. A public company must end with the suffix 'public limited company' or the Welsh equivalent 'cwmni cyhoeddus cyfyngedig' or the abbreviation 'plc' or 'ccc' (s 58 of the CA 2006). A private company must end with the word 'limited' or the Welsh equivalent 'cyfyngedig' or 'ltd' or 'cyf' or, alternatively, 'unlimited' or 'anghyfyngedig' (s 59 of the CA 2006).

The fundamental distinction between the private and the public company (see diagram on p. 9 for example) is that the private company is prohibited from seeking finance from the general public by offering its shares or debentures to the public and it is a criminal offence for its shares to be advertised. The public company by contrast may seek finance in this way.

The CA 2006 and other pieces of legislation are peppered with a variety of other distinctions. Some of these are as follows:

- A private company need have only one director; a public company must have at least two (s 154 of the CA 2006).

- The minimum membership of both public and private companies can now be one (s 24 CA 1985 was repealed from October 2008).

- The company secretary of a public company must have a recognised professional qualification; private companies no longer need to have a company secretary but need to notify Companies House if they choose to dispense with a company secretary.

- Before a public company may pay a dividend, it must ensure not only that it has trading profits but also that its capital assets are maintained in value to at least the value of the subscribed share capital plus undistributable reserves (s 831 of the CA 2006). There is no such statutory rule imposing such a need on a private company.

- Private companies can now take advantage of the audit exemption.

- Private companies may purchase their own shares in order to reduce capital (s 678 of the CA 2006). Private companies may also give financial assistance to purchase their own shares (s 679 of the CA 2006). Public companies are still prevented from doing either of these things.

- The elective resolution regime was repealed by CA 2006. Private companies are no longer required to hold annual general meetings. For public companies the AGM must be held within six months of the year end (s 336 of the CA 2006) with a minimum of 21 clear days' notice given.

- Private companies may act by unanimous written resolution in most cases; there is no such formal provision for public companies.

- There is now a minimum age of 16 for directors in both public and private companies. The requirements relating to the appointment of directors aged 70 or over to the board of a public company have now been abolished.

There are other distinctions between private and public companies but these represent some of the better-known differences. However, the idea of separate legislation for public companies and private companies was rejected. (See diagram (a), opposite.)

Companies can be classified in other ways (see diagram (b), opposite, for example).

PARTNERSHIPS

We have briefly met some of the differences between partnerships and companies. It is worth noting that in the same way as there are different types of companies, there are also different forms of partnerships.

PARTNERSHIP ACT 1890

The Partnership Act sets out the basic rules for setting up a business of this type and is important as in the absence of a Partnership Agreement, it is the provisions of the Act which will be applied. The definition of a partnership is found in s 1 where it is stated that a partnership is 'the relation which subsists between persons carrying on a business in common with a view of profit.' The

Classifications of companies

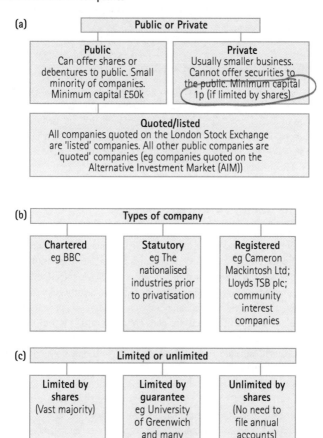

(a)

Public or Private

Public
Can offer shares or debentures to public. Small minority of companies. Minimum capital £50k

Private
Usually smaller business. Cannot offer securities to the public. Minimum capital 1p (if limited by shares)

Quoted/listed
All companies quoted on the London Stock Exchange are 'listed' companies. All other public companies are 'quoted' companies (eg companies quoted on the Alternative Investment Market (AIM))

(b)

Types of company

Chartered
eg BBC

Statutory
eg The nationalised industries prior to privatisation

Registered
eg Cameron Mackintosh Ltd; Lloyds TSB plc; community interest companies

(c)

Limited or unlimited

Limited by shares
(Vast majority)

Limited by guarantee
eg University of Greenwich and many other charitable organisations

Unlimited by shares
(No need to file annual accounts)

relationship must be contractual but the business does not have to have started trading. The partnership should also be between persons so it would be possible to have a company as a partner as companies can be legal persons. Partners have the right to be in management of the business because partners are required to act in common. Finally, the statement that there should be a view of profit does not require the partnership to share profits (*M Young Legal Associates Ltd v Zahid Solicitors* (a firm) [2006]).

LIMITED PARTNERSHIP ACT 1907

This a special, and relatively rare, form of partnership in which one or more partner has limited liability for the business' debts. The liability is limited to the amount of capital initially invested. This type of partnership is used mainly by institutional investors and venture capitalists. It is not a legal entity but it can have an unlimited number of members. Limited partnerships must be registered with the Registrar of Companies.

LIMITED LIABILITY PARTNERSHIPS

Under the Limited Liability Partnerships Act (LLPA) 2000, it is possible to create a different form of business association, called a limited liability partnership (LLP). Under the LLPA 2000, an LLP becomes a corporate body with a legal personality separate from that of its members. It follows therefore that the members of an LLP will not ordinarily become liable for the debts of the LLP and, although an LLP is likely to have features similar to an ordinary partnership, the law relating to ordinary partnerships does not apply to LLPs (s 1 of the LLPA 2000). To be incorporated, an LLP needs to be registered with the registrar of companies at Companies House. Many of the detailed provisions relating to LLPs are to be found in secondary legislation, in particular the Limited Liability Partnership Regulations (LLPR) 2001. These regulations apply a number of provisions from the CA 2006 and Insolvency Act 1986 to LLPs, with some modification to reflect the different nature of an LLP. Since the LLPA 2000 came into force (on 6 April 2001), a number of firms, such as solicitors and accountants, have chosen to register as LLPs.

FORMATION OF AN LLP

An LLP is created by registration with the registrar of companies. Once the registrar has registered an LLP and issued a certificate of incorporation, a new corporate body, with a legal personality of its own, is created. Section 2(1) of the LLPA 2000 provides that:

> Two or more persons associated for carrying on a lawful business with a view to profit must have subscribed their names to an incorporation document which is to be delivered to the registrar of companies.

A statement that the requirements of s 2 of the LLPA 2000 have been complied with is also delivered to the registrar of companies. This statement must be made by one of the subscribers to the incorporation document or by a solicitor who was engaged in the formation of the LLP.

The incorporation document is to be in a form approved by the registrar of companies and to state the name of the LLP, whether the registered office is in England and Wales, in Wales or in Scotland; the address of the LLP; the names and addresses of all the members on incorporation; and a statement of who the designated members are or a statement that all members of the LLP, at any time, are to be designated members. The incorporation document can be submitted electronically.

MEMBERS AND DESIGNATED MEMBERS

Section 4(1) of the LLPA 2000 provides that the members of an LLP are the persons who subscribed to the incorporation document. Section 4(2) of the LLPA 2000 provides that any other person may become a member by agreement with all existing members and s 4(3) of the LLPA 2000 provides that a person may cease to be a member either by agreement with the other members or by giving reasonable notice to the other members. A member who has died, or become dissolved in the case of a corporate member, ceases to be a member.

The LLPA 2000 provides for two members to become designated members who are responsible for the LLP complying with the administrative requirements laid down by the LLPR 2001. Where there is no designated member, or only one designated member, every member of the LLP becomes a designated member (s 8(2) of the LLPA 2000). A person who ceases to be a member of an LLP ceases to be a designated member.

Designated members have certain specific duties such as signing and delivery to the registrar the LLP's accounts and annual return; giving the registrar notice that an LLP has changed its name or who are its designated members. The rules

11

on the approval and removal of auditors, the filing of an annual return and on the filing of accounts are mainly the same as those which apply to companies.

The filing of accounts the annual return and the maintaining of registers, etc, can be done electronically.

CONTRACTUAL AND TORTIOUS LIABILITY

Section 6(1) of the LLPA 2000 provides that every member of the LLP is an agent of the LLP and therefore an LLP will be bound by a contract entered into by an agent with authority to make it. However, under s 6(2) of the LLPA 2000, an LLP is not bound by anything done by a member in dealing with a person where (i) the member in fact has no authority to act for the LLP by doing that thing and (ii) the person knows that he has no authority or does not know or believe him to be a member of the LLP.

Section 51 of the CA 2006 applies to LLPs so a person making a pre-incorporation contract on behalf of an LLP will be liable on it. Under s 5(2) of the LLPA 2000, an agreement made before the incorporation of an LLP between the subscribers to the incorporation document may impose obligations on the LLP to take effect at any time after its incorporation.

Under s 4(4) of the LLPA 2000 an LLP is liable for any wrongful act or omission of a member committed during the course of the business of the LLP or with the authority of the LLP. Where a member is liable for any wrongful act or omission, the LLP will be liable equally.

MEMBERS' RELATIONSHIP WITH EACH OTHER

Section 5(1) of the LLPA 2000 provides that the mutual rights and duties of the members of an LLP as between each other, and as between the members and the LLP, shall be governed by agreement between the members or between the LLP and the members. It is likely that such an agreement will be based on terms similar to those found in an ordinary partnership. In the absence of any agreement, the default provisions of Regulation 7 of the LLPR 2001 will apply. These are similar to the default provisions set out in s 24 of the PA 1890.

Regulation 8 of the LLPR 2001 provides that no majority can expel any member unless a power to do so has been conferred by express agreement between the members. If a member is expelled, as with an ordinary partnership, the power must be exercised in good faith for the benefit of the LLP.

MINORITY PROTECTION

Under s 122(1) of the Insolvency Act (IA) 1986, a member of an LLP can petition the court for a winding up order on the ground that it is just and equitable and s 994 of the CA 2006 enables a member to petition the court for relief on the ground of unfair prejudice, such as wrongful exclusion from management.

The circumstances in which the Department of Trade and Industry can investigate a company's affairs apply also to LLPs. Such an investigation can arise where a court orders an investigation or where at least 20 members of the LLP request an investigation.

WINDING UP

The IA 1986 applies to LLPs in the same way that it applies to companies and, as an LLP is a corporate body, the LLP will be liable for any debts incurred and not generally its members.

However, the wrongful trading and fraudulent trading provisions under ss 213 and 214 of the IA 1986 apply to members of an LLP, so that, on a winding up of an LLP, a court can order a member to contribute to the assets of the LLP. Members can also be made liable under ss 74 and 214A of the IA 1986. Section 74 of the IA 1986 provides that members of an LLP can agree to assume liability for the company's debts. Section 214A of the IA 1986 provides that a member or shadow member who within two years of the commencement of winding up, withdrew LLP property while having reasonable grounds for believing either that the LLP could not pay its debts or would have been unable to pay its debts once the property had been withdrawn, can be ordered by a court on an application by the liquidator to pay such a contribution to the LLP's assets as the court thinks proper. A shadow member is a person in accordance with whose directions or instructions the members of a LLP are accustomed to act, other than advice given in a professional capacity.

DISQUALIFICATION OF MEMBERS

The Company Directors Disqualification Act (CDDA) 1986 applies to both members and shadow members of an LLP, so that a person disqualified from being a director of a company or a member of an LLP will be disqualified from being a director or a member of any company. A person who acts as an LLP member in breach of a disqualification order or undertaking commits a criminal offence and can be made liable for the LLP's debts.

CORPORATE PERSONALITY

It is commonplace in examinations for there to be a question on the principle of separate legal personality of the company. The most important case on corporate personality in English company law is *Salomon v Salomon & Co Ltd* [1897], although the principle of separate corporate personality was recognised before its consequences were brought home in this landmark case. The facts of this case were that Salomon had incorporated his boot and shoe repair business, transferring it to a company. He took all the shares of the company except six which were held by his wife, daughter and four sons. Part of the payment for the transfer of the business was made in the form of debentures (a secured loan) issued by the company to Salomon. Salomon transferred the debentures to Broderip in exchange for a loan. Salomon defaulted on payment of interest on the loan and Broderip sought to enforce the security against the company. Unsecured creditors tried to put the company into liquidation. A dispute ensued as to whether Broderip or the 14 unsecured creditors had priority in relation to payment of the debts. It was argued for the unsecured creditors that Salomon's security was void as the company was a sham and was in reality the agent of Salomon. The House of Lords held that this was not the case and the company had been properly incorporated and that therefore the security was valid and could be enforced.

The case is the most important case in company law since it is from this case that many of the principles of English company law flow. However, the spirit of the decision has not been universally followed and there are exceptions to the *Salomon* principle where the corporate veil is lifted. Before turning to the exceptions, it is worth noting some further applications of the basic principle. In *Lee v Lee's Air Farming Ltd* [1961], a Privy Council case from New Zealand, Mrs Lee was the widow of Mr Lee, the governing director of a company, who owned all of the shares except one and who, as chief pilot, was killed on company business flying the company's plane. Mrs Lee was able to argue that her husband, in his capacity as a pilot, was an employee and thus secured a pension from the New Zealand Workman's Compensation Fund. The *Salomon* principle was thus applied. In *Macaura v Northern Assurance Co Ltd* [1925], similarly, such an argument prevailed. In this case, however, it was not in the interest of the shareholder concerned that the principle applied. The majority shareholder had continued to insure timber, which he had sold to the company and which was destroyed by fire, in his own name. The insurance company argued successfully that it was not his timber but that of the company. In *Gramophone and Typewriter Ltd v Stanley* [1908], the court held that the business of the company was not the business of the members.

In *Lonrho Ltd v Shell Petroleum Co Ltd* [1980], we have another example of the application of the *Salomon* principle. In this case, Lonrho sought discovery of documents held by a subsidiary of Shell Petroleum in southern Africa. The House of Lords held that the order for discovery did not extend to the subsidiary since this was a separate company.

There was a restatement of the basic *Salomon* principle in *Adams v Cape Industries plc* [1990]. It was noted by the Court of Appeal, *per* Slade LJ:

> . . . saving cases which turn on the wording of particular statutes or contracts, the court is not free to disregard the principle of *Salomon v Salomon & Company Ltd* [1897] merely because it considers that justice so requires.

This approach was confirmed in *Ord v Belhaven Pubs Ltd* [1998]; *Yukong Lines Ltd of Korea v Rendsburg Investments Corp of Liberia* [1998]; *Re Polly Peck International plc* [1996]; and *Trustor AB v Smallbone (No 2)* [2001].

In tackling a question on the area of corporate personality, care should be taken to ensure that your answer corresponds with the question that is asked. Sometimes, the question will ask merely for a discussion about the statutory exceptions to the *Salomon* principle, for example, 'Often, Parliament has intervened to mitigate the effect of the *Salomon* principle. Discuss'. On other occasions, the question will be phrased in such a way that both statutory and judicial exceptions should be discussed, for example, 'On occasion, the courts and

15

Parliament have intervened to mitigate the effects of the *Salomon* doctrine. Discuss'.

STATUTORY EXCEPTIONS

There are various statutory provisions which remove the advantages of forming a company, particularly that of limited liability:

- Section 767(3) of the CA 2006 provides that where a public company fails to obtain a trading certificate, in addition to its certificate of incorporation, before trading and borrowing money, the company's directors are liable for any obligations incurred.

- Sections 398–408 of the CA 2006 provide that where a group situation exists (that is, where there is a holding company and subsidiaries), then group accounts should be prepared. In assessing whether this is the case, the veil is being lifted to determine if a holding company–subsidiary company relationship exists (see the definition of holding and subsidiary companies in ss 1159 and 1160 of the CA 2006).

- Section 994 of the CA 2006 may involve lifting the veil to determine, for example, the basis on which the company was formed (see *Re London School of Electronics* [1986]).

- Sections 1159 and 1160 of the CA 2006 set out the formula for determining if a holding company–subsidiary company relationship exists.

- Section 15 of the Company Directors Disqualification Act 1986 provides that if a director who is disqualified continues to act as a director he will be personally liable for the debts and obligations of the company.

- Section 122(1)(g) of the IA 1986 provides that a petitioner may present a petition to wind the company up on the just and equitable ground. On occasion, this may be based on a situation involving lifting of the veil, as in *Ebrahimi v Westbourne Galleries Ltd* [1973], where the petitioner was pointing to the basis on which the company had been formed.

- Section 213 of the IA 1986 (relating to fraudulent trading) provides that where a person trades through the medium of a company knowing, for example, that the company is unable to pay its debts as they fall due, he may be held liable to make contributions to the company's assets. This has a criminal counterpart in s 993(1) of the CA 2006.

▨ Section 214 of the IA 1986 (relating to wrongful trading) provides that where a director or shadow director ought to know that the company is unable to pay its debts as they fall due, he may be held liable to make a contribution to the company's assets where the company is being wound up.

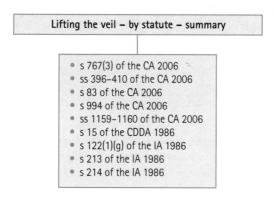

Lifting the veil – by statute – summary

- s 767(3) of the CA 2006
- ss 396–410 of the CA 2006
- s 83 of the CA 2006
- s 994 of the CA 2006
- ss 1159–1160 of the CA 2006
- s 15 of the CDDA 1986
- s 122(1)(g) of the IA 1986
- s 213 of the IA 1986
- s 214 of the IA 1986

JUDICIAL EXCEPTIONS

In addition to the statutory exceptions to the *Salomon* principle, there are judicial decisions where the veil is lifted.

It is not easy to categorise these cases but there are some consistent themes which can be singled out. One of these is to combat fraud.

COMBATING FRAUD

In *Jones v Lipman* [1962], a vendor had agreed to sell a piece of land. Subsequently, he changed his mind. In an effort to defeat a move to obtain specific performance, the vendor transferred the land to a company which he controlled. The court refused to countenance this. The veil was lifted and specific performance was ordered against the vendor and the company.

In *Gilford Motor Co Ltd v Horne* [1933], an employee had entered into an agreement not to compete with his former employer after ceasing employment. In order to try to avoid this restriction, the employee set up a company and acted through that. The court held that this manoeuvre would not be tolerated, the veil would be lifted and an injunction would be issued against the company too.

These cases involve fraud in the sense that the company is being used to avoid an *existing* contractual obligation. The Court of Appeal stated in *Adams v Cape Industries plc* [1990] that the veil would not be lifted simply on the ground that the company was formed to avoid *future* obligations and liabilities.

There are other examples of the veil being lifted to combat fraud: see *Re Darby ex p Brougham* [1911]; *Re FG (Films) Ltd* [1953]; *Re Bugle Press* [1961]; *Wallersteiner v Moir* [1974]; and *Trustor AB v Smallbone (No 2)* [2001].

AGENCY

Another theme which runs through the cases is agency. Often, the veil will be lifted where a relationship of agency is found to exist.

In *Salomon* itself, agency, in the sense that the company was the agent of the shareholder, had been rejected by the House of Lords. (See also *Adams v Cape Industries plc* [1990] on this point.)

In *Smith, Stone and Knight Ltd v Birmingham Corp* [1939], Atkinson J lifted the veil to enable a subsidiary company operating a business on land owned by the holding company to claim compensation on the ground of agency.

In *Firestone Tyre and Rubber Co Ltd v Llewellin* [1957], agency was once again the trigger for lifting the veil where a British company manufacturing tyres for an American holding company was held to be its agent. In *Re FG (Films) Ltd* [1953], where fraud or sharp practice was also a factor, the American holding company set up a British subsidiary to produce the film 'Monsoon'. It was held that there was an agency relationship and that the film was an American one.

GROUPS OF COMPANIES

This is governed by s 1159 of the CA 2006 which shifts the emphasis from ownership of shares to control of shares. The common law is demonstrated by cases such as *Harold Holdsworth & Co (Wakefield) Ltd v Caddies* [1955], where the respondent held an employment contract with the appellant company to serve it as managing director. The House of Lords held that the appellant company could require the respondent to serve a subsidiary company.

The case that is widely seen as the leading case in this area is *DHN Food Distributors Ltd v Tower Hamlets London Borough Council* [1976]. Like *Smith, Stone and Knight Ltd v Birmingham Corp* [1939], the case concerned compensation for compulsory purchase. In the *DHN* case, the company operating the business was the holding company and the premises were owned by the company's wholly owned subsidiary. Like *Smith, Stone and Knight Ltd*, compensation was only payable for disturbance of the business if the business was operated on land owned by the company.

However, it is not every wholly owned subsidiary that is identified with its holding company. It did not happen, for example, in *Lonrho Ltd v Shell Petroleum Co Ltd* [1980] and the House of Lords in *Woolfson v Strathclyde Regional Council* [1978] and the Court of Appeal in *Adams v Cape Industries plc* [1990], cast serious doubt on the correctness of the judgment of Lord Denning in the *DHN* case.

TRUST

The concept of the trust has also been utilised on occasion to circumvent the corporate facade. In *Trebanog Working Men's Club v Macdonald* [1940], the club was charged with selling liquor without a licence. It was held by the divisional court that the club held the liquor on trust for its members so there was no offence.

In *The Abbey, Malvern Wells Ltd v Ministry of Local Government and Planning* [1951], it was held that shares in a company were held on trust and that those directing the affairs of the company were trustees so that the court could lift the veil and impose the terms of the trust on the company's property.

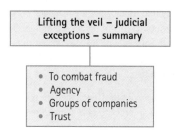

Lifting the veil – judicial exceptions – summary
• To combat fraud
• Agency
• Groups of companies
• Trust

CORPORATE KILLING

CORPORATE MANSLAUGHTER

The courts have accepted that it is possible for a company to be guilty of manslaughter by an unlawful act or gross negligence (*R v P and O European Ferries (Dover) Ltd* [1990]). However, because criminal acts require not just the *actus reus* (the act) but also the *mens rea* (guilty mind), it has been difficult to bring successful prosecutions against companies. Effectively this has meant that an individual has had to be identified as being the 'controlling mind' of the company. While this approach worked with small companies which were owned and operated by one person, it resulted in failure when applied to larger companies because the controlling mind could not be identified, even if it was a general failing of policy or procedures within the company which led to the death. To remedy this situation the Corporate Manslaughter and Corporate Homicide Act 2007 was passed. Now under s 1 of the Act the offence of Corporate Manslaughter is committed by a company if the way in which its activities are managed or organised: (a) causes a person's death; and (b) amounts to a gross breach of a relevant duty of care owed by the company to that person. This has now been tested in the case of *R v Cotswold Geotechnical Holdings* [2011]. However, despite the success in finding the company to be guilty and imposing a fine of £385,000, as the company was run by a sole director it is submitted that the law still requires real testing on a substantially larger company with a complex management structure. It has also proved to be a pyrrhic victory as the company went into voluntary liquidation shortly after leave to appeal against conviction and sentence was refused.

This still remains a complex and difficult offence to establish as 'gross breach' is defined in s 1(4)(b) as conduct falling below what could be reasonably expected of the company in the circumstances. Additionally, a company is only guilty of the offence if the way that its activities are managed or organised by its senior management is a substantial part of the breach of duty. Section 1(4)(c) defines senior management as persons who play significant roles in making decisions about how the company's activities are run or do the actual managing or organising of those activities.

If a company is found guilty of the offence, then the punishment is a fine, which may be accompanied by an order to take steps to remedy the breach of duty which caused the death.

CONCLUSION

This is a favourite examination topic. It is a straightforward area and, although there is no magic categorisation of the judicial exceptions, it is likely that the categorisation set out here will be helpful. In preparing to answer a question on this area, pay particular attention to the facts of the main cases. Spice your answers up with academic citation from other sources. Above all else, be sure to read the examination question carefully and tailor your answer accordingly.

You should now be confident that you would be able to tick all of the boxes on the checklist at the beginning of this chapter. To check your knowledge of Incorporation why not visit the companion website and take the Multiple Choice Question test. Check your understanding of the terms and vocabulary used in this chapter with the flashcard glossary.

The company's constitution

2

INTRODUCTION

This chapter will look at certain areas in depth, concentrating on those that are considered to be essential. It should be remembered that many amendments have been made to constitutional arrangements of a company under the Companies Act 2006 and came into effect from 2009.

APPLICATION FOR REGISTRATION

Under the CA 2006, the importance of a company's memorandum of association was reduced to mere historical record. Constitutional provisions are now located in the Articles of Association instead. The memorandum is a document that needs to be submitted as part of the incorporation process and will not be capable of amendment. The information that was formerly contained in the memorandum will now be provided to the Registrar in an application for registration under s 9 of the CA 2006. The application for registration must state:

- the name of the company (s 9(2));
- situation of the company's registered office (s 9(2));
- whether the liability of members is to be limited, and if so whether it is to be limited by shares or guarantee (s 9(2));
- whether the company is to be private or public (s 9(2)).

The application for registration must also contain:

- a statement of initial shareholding
- statement of share capital
- statement of guarantee
- statement of proposed officers
- statement of compliance

OBJECTS CLAUSES AND *ULTRA VIRES*

This is an area that has been amended by the introduction of the Companies Act 2006. Now by virtue of s 31 of the CA 2006 unless a company's articles specifically restrict the objects of the company, its objects are unrestricted. If the company does decide to amend its objects, then this change must be made via amendment of the articles. The law is now stated in s 39 of the CA 2006. The effect of the new law is to pretty much abolish *ultra vires*. However, there are still occasions when a challenge could arise. These are where a director or connected person is involved or a third party acted in bad faith. A challenge could also arise if an injunction is sought to prevent directors acting or to allege a breach of duty after events. Section 239 of the CA 2006 requires only an ordinary resolution to ratify any breaches of duty by directors. However, the votes of any director or connected person involved in the breach of duty will not count. Section 41(3) of the CA 2006 makes any directors involved liable to account for the transaction and to indemnify the company whether they knew they were exceeding their powers or not.

THE POSITION AT COMMON LAW

The old case is still applicable in certain limited circumstances. Prior to statutory reform, at common law, contracts that were outside the scope of the company's objects clause were *ultra vires* and void. Before statutory intervention, there-fore, the question was relatively simple. If the objects clause covered the rele-vant contract it was valid, if it was outside the company's permitted range of activities it was void and unenforceable (see *Ashbury Railway Carriage & Iron Co Ltd v Riche* [1875]).

In *Cotman v Brougham* [1918] the company's memorandum had been drafted to contain over 30 sub-clauses to avoid the application of the 'main object rule'. Following this case many companies had memoranda drafted in similar fashion. This was further developed in *Bell Houses Ltd v City Wall Properties Ltd* [1966] with the use of a 'subjective clause'. This type of clause allowed the company to carry on any other trade or business whatsoever which could in the opinion of the board of directors be advantageously carried on by the company in connec-tion with or as ancillary to any of the above businesses or the general business of the company.

CONCLUSION

You should make sure that you are familiar with the law as it now stands under CA 2006 and the history behind the changes.

COMPANY NAME

Some knowledge of the rules governing the choice of name for a company is helpful. Although it is rare for there to be a specific question on the company name, it may feature as part of a problem question, particularly as this area has been subject to reform and consolidation under the CA 2006.

We have already met the requirement under s 9 of the CA 2006 that the application for registration must state the company's proposed name. Further rules relating to company names are set out in Part 5 of the CA 2006. These sections provide as follows:

▓ Section 58 of the CA 2006 provides that the name of a public company must end with the words 'public limited company' or the recognised abbreviation 'plc' or the Welsh equivalent 'cwmni cyhoeddus cyfyngedig' or 'ccc'. By contrast, s 59 of the CA 2006 states that a private company limited by shares or by guarantee should end with 'limited' or the recognised abbreviation 'Ltd' or the Welsh equivalent 'cyfyngedig' or 'cyf'. Sometimes, a private limited company may be permitted to omit the word 'limited' from the end of its name. Sections 60–64 of the CA 2006 allow companies to omit the word 'limited' on satisfying certain conditions. The company concerned must be a private limited company and have as its objects the promotion of commerce, art, science, education, religion, charity or any profession, and anything incidental or conducive to any of those objects and must have a requirement in its constitution that its profits or other income be applied in promoting those objects. The constitution must also prohibit the payment of dividends to its members and require all of the assets which would otherwise be available to its members generally to be transferred on its winding up to another body with similar objects or to a body the objects of which are the promotion of charity and anything incidental or conducive thereto. Where such an exemption from using the word 'limited' is desired, then a statutory declaration that a company complies with the above requirements must be delivered to the registrar of companies who may accept the declaration as evidence of the matters stated in it. The registrar may refuse to register a company by a name which does not include the word 'limited' unless such a declaration has been delivered to him (if the company is limited).

▨ Section 53 of the CA 2006 prohibits the use of certain names. The words 'public limited company', 'limited' and 'unlimited' can only be used at the end of the company name, as may the Welsh equivalents 'cwmni cyhoeddus cyfyngedig', 'cyfyngedig' and 'anghyfyngedig' respectively. The same principle applies to the recognised abbreviations of these words or expressions. Names which would in the opinion of the Secretary of State constitute a criminal offence or which in the opinion of the Secretary of State would be offensive are also forbidden (s 53 of the CA 2006). Certain words may only be used with the approval of the Secretary of State. If the name in the opinion of the Secretary of State would be likely to give the impression that the company is connected with Her Majesty's Government or a local authority, approval is needed (s 54 of the CA 2006).

▨ Section 66 of the CA 2006 requires that the name must not be the same as a name already appearing on the index of company names kept by the registrar of companies under s 1099 of the CA 2006 (s 53 of the CA 2006). If a name should be registered by the registrar and it is subsequently discovered that the name is the same as an existing name or too similar to an existing name or a name that should have appeared on the index at that time, then the Secretary of State can, within 12 months of the registration, require the company to change its name (s 77 of the CA 2006).

▨ There are certain words and expressions that require the prior permission of either the Secretary of State or some other designated body (s 55 of the CA 2006). There is a list of such words in regulations made under s 55 of the CA 2006. If the name of the company implies some regional, national or international pre-eminence, governmental link or sponsorship or some pre-eminent status, then consent may well be required. Thus, if it is desired to use the word 'University', the consent of the Privy Council would be needed. In seeking registration of the company name, it would be appropriate to have copies of the letters sent to the relevant body and the response indicating that there is no objection.

The choice of company name is limited by other considerations. If the name constitutes a registered trademark, the person who has the trademark may institute summary proceedings to prevent use of the name under the Trade Marks Act 1994.

▨ The use of the name which is already used by an existing business (whether sole trader, partnership or company) or a name which is similar to that of an existing business such as it appears to the trading public that there is a link between the two businesses may be subject to a passing off action in tort which if successful will involve the granting of an injunction to prevent further use of the name and an account of profits in respect of the past use of the name. In *Ewing v Buttercup Margarine Co Ltd* [1917], Astbury J, affirmed by the Court of Appeal, held that the plaintiff who operated the Buttercup Dairy Company could obtain an injunction against the Buttercup Margarine Company since this name was calculated to deceive, by diverting customers or potential customers from the plaintiff to the defendant. Less obviously, in *Chill Foods (Scotland) Ltd v Cool Foods Ltd* [1977], Murray and Dick had run a company called S and J Catering Products Ltd (S and J) which acquired a company called Chill Foods (Scotland) Ltd (Chill Foods). Dick then founded a company called Cool Foods Ltd trading in the same areas as S and J and Chill Foods. An interdict was granted preventing Cool Foods Ltd from trading because of the similarity of name, similarity of business and the similarity of trading areas. It is not automatic that an injunction will be granted even where a business has an identical name. There must clearly be some similarity in the trading area and the business concern. Thus, in *Tussaud v Tussaud* [1890], Madame Tussaud and Sons Ltd were granted an injunction to restrain Louis Tussaud Ltd from carrying on a similar business, namely a waxworks exhibition in Shaftesbury Avenue, which was clearly similar to the one 'so long and successfully carried on in Baker Street and the Marylebone Road'.

▨ A novel, if unsuccessful, argument was deployed in *Exxon Corp v Exxon Insurance Consultants International Ltd* [1982] where the claimant claimed copyright in the word 'Exxon' as an original literary work under s 2 of the Copyright Act 1956. The Court of Appeal held that the single word could not qualify as an original literary work so the defendant could not be restrained from using it on the grounds of breach of copyright.

▨ In an attempt to avoid the so called 'Phoenix syndrome' where controllers of a company put it into insolvent liquidation, thereby releasing the business from existing debts, and then incorporate a new company with the same or a similar name, s 216 of the Insolvency Act (IA) 1986 makes it a criminal offence for a director of an insolvent company to be a director of a new company with the same name or a name which suggests an association with the insolvent company within five years of the insolvency. Further, s 217 of the IA 1986 imposes personal liability on the director for the debts of the new company (see *Thorne v Silverleaf* [1994]).

CHOICE OF COMPANY NAME – SUMMARY CHANGE OF NAME

- Check name has not already been used.
- Name must not be offensive.
- Name must not constitute a criminal offence, eg unauthorised use of 'Red Cross'.
- Some words need special authority, eg Windsor, Medical, University.
- Name must not infringe a trade mark.
- The tort of passing off restricts the use of a name used by other businesses.
- Note the 'Phoenix syndrome' provisions.

Section 77 of the CA 2006 provides that a company may change its name by special resolution in general meeting. The same rules apply on a change of name as apply to the initial choice of name.

Sometimes, the Secretary of State may require a change of name. It has already been noted that if he finds that the name is too similar to an existing name he may require a change within 12 months (s 77(2) of the CA 2006). This applies in just the same way after a name has been changed as on a choice of name on initial incorporation.

If a company provides misleading information to the registrar on incorporation or on a change of a name, the registrar may order a change within five years (s 75 of the CA 2006).

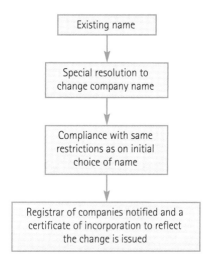

The Secretary of State may also require an alteration of name if he believes that it gives a misleading indication of the nature or activities of the company so as to be likely to cause harm to the public. This power may be exercised at any time (s 76(1) of the CA 2006). The direction must be complied with within six weeks.

ARTICLES OF ASSOCIATION

The articles of association is now the most important document to be submitted to the registrar (s 18 of the CA 2006). Although a company must have articles of association, the contents of the articles are not laid down by the CA 2006. Under s 20 of the CA 2006 a limited company does not have to register articles. If this is the case, then the model articles will apply (Companies (Model Articles) Regulations 2008, SI 2008/3229). The simplified format reflects the lifting of administrative burden on small companies.

ALTERATION OF THE ARTICLES

One change to note is under s 22 of the CA 2006 which gives a company the power to entrench provisions in the articles. However, entrenched provisions are not irreversible; they are merely subject to more restrictive procedures for amendment or repeal than non-entrenched provisions.

Section 21 of the CA 2006 provides that a company may by special resolution alter its articles. A company may not be injuncted where it has agreed not to alter its articles (see *Punt v Symons & Co* [1903]). In fact, this power to alter the articles of association of a company is subject to various restrictions:

▪ The company cannot alter its articles to contravene the provisions of the Companies Act. For example, a provision in the articles which seeks to exempt an officer of the company from liability for negligence would be void by virtue of s 532 of the CA 2006. In the same way, a provision seeking to increase the liability of a member beyond that of his original contractual obligation is void by virtue of s 25 of the CA 2006. Section 16(1) provides:

> . . . a member of a company is not bound by an alteration made in the memorandum or articles after the date on which he became a member, if and so far as the alteration:
>
> (a) requires him to take or subscribe for more shares than the number held by him at the date on which the alteration is made; or
> (b) in any way increases his liability as at that date to contribute to the company's share capital or otherwise to pay money to the company.

▪ If an alteration of the articles is proposed which conflicts with an order of the court, this is void. For example, an order of the court under s 996 of the CA 2006 relating to the remedy for unfairly prejudicial conduct cannot be overridden by a change of articles.

▪ If the proposed alteration of articles involves an alteration or abrogation of class rights, special procedures have to be followed in addition to the passing of a special resolution as required under s 21 of the CA 2006. The company must follow the regime which is appropriate to the variation of class rights which is set out in ss 630–634 of the CA 2006.

Class rights

If the change of articles also involves a variation of class rights an additional procedure must be followed. If the company has more than one class of share,

31

questions of variation of class rights sometimes arise. Generally, it will be obvious if there is more than one class of share, as the shares will generally have a label attached to them, for example, ordinary shares or preference shares. However, it is not always so simple. On occasion, if particular rights attach to a certain shareholding, this might constitute those shares as a separate class of shares. This was held to be the position in *Cumbrian Newspapers Group Ltd v Cumberland and Westmorland Herald Newspaper and Printing Co Ltd* [1987].

> ### ▶ CUMBRIAN NEWSPAPERS GROUP LTD v CUMBERLAND AND WESTMORLAND HERALD NEWSPAPER AND PRINTING CO LTD [1987]

The claimant company, Cumbrian Newspapers Ltd, was the holder of 10.67 per cent of the issued ordinary shares of the defendant company, Cumberland and Westmorland Herald Newspaper and Printing Company Ltd. The defendant company's articles provided, *inter alia*, for a right of pre-emption over any shares which were being transferred in favour of the claimant. Furthermore, Art 12 in the articles of association provided that:

... if and so long as Cumberland Newspapers Ltd should be registered as the holder of not less than one-tenth in nominal value of the issued ordinary share capital of the company, Cumberland Newspapers Ltd shall be entitled from time to time to nominate one person to be a director of the company.

Scott J held that the shares held by Cumbrian Newspapers Group constituted a separate class of shares and, therefore, the right to nominate a director was a right attached to a class of shares.

The case is important because it demonstrates that different rights differentiate classes of shares and the breadth of rights that can be attached to shares.

In that case, the claimant company, Cumbrian Newspapers Ltd, was the holder of 10.67 per cent of the issued ordinary shares of the defendant company,

Cumberland and Westmorland Herald Newspaper and Printing Company Ltd. The defendant company's articles provided, *inter alia*, for a right of pre-emption over any shares which were being transferred in favour of the claimant. Furthermore, Art 12 in the articles of association provided that:

... if and so long as Cumberland Newspapers Ltd should be registered as the holder of not less than one-tenth in nominal value of the issued ordinary share capital of the company, Cumberland Newspapers Ltd shall be entitled from time to time to nominate one person to be a director of the company.

Scott J held that the shares held by Cumbrian Newspapers Group constituted a separate class of shares and, therefore, the right to nominate a director was a right attached to a class of shares.

Once it has been determined that there is more than one class of share in the company, the next question for determination is whether there has been a variation of the rights attaching to those shares. Once again, this may not be as straightforward as it at first appears. By contrast with the question of whether there is more than one class of share, the approach of the courts here is somewhat restrictive. The question had to be considered, for example, in *Greenhalgh v Arderne Cinemas Ltd* [1946]. In this case, the company had two classes of shares: 50 pence shares and 10 pence shares. The 50 pence shares carried one vote each as did the 10 pence shares. The resolution that was proposed was to sub-divide the 50 pence shares into 10 pence shares thus giving the shares in effect five times as many votes as previously. It was argued on behalf of the 10 pence shareholders that this constituted a variation of class rights and that their rights were being varied. The Court of Appeal took the view that this did not constitute a variation. The rights attaching to the 10 pence shares remained constant. They carried one vote per share. Such an approach is restrictive. Furthermore, it seems from the judgment of Lord Greene MR that, had the approach been to limit the votes of the 10 pence shares to one vote for every five shares of that class, this would have been a variation. Lord Greene MR said:

Of course, if it had been attempted to reduce that voting right, for example, by providing or attempting to provide that there should be one vote for every five of such shares, that would have been an interference with the voting rights attached to that class of shares. But

33

> nothing of the kind has been done; the right to have one vote per share is left undisturbed.

With respect to the learned judge, something of the kind *had* been done. The practical effect of quintupling the votes of the 50 pence shareholders is precisely the same as dividing the votes of the 10 pence shareholders by five. The approach is excessively legalistic.

Furthermore, in *House of Fraser plc v ACGE Investments Ltd* [1987], it was held that the repayment and cancellation of preference shares on a reduction of capital was not an alteration or variation of the class rights of the preference shareholders.

Once it has been established that there has been a variation of class rights, the rules that have to be followed to carry the variation into effect are dependent upon whether the company has a share capital or not. If a company has a share capital then the rights may be varied:

(a) in accordance with provision in the company's articles for the variation of those rights, or

(b) where the company's articles contain no such provision, if the members of that class consent to the variation in accordance with s 630 (2) and (4) CA 2006.

The consent required for the purposes of s 630 on the part of the members of a class is:

(a) consent in writing from at least three-quarters of the members of the class, or

(b) a special resolution passed at a separate general meeting of the members of that class sanctioning the variation.

If the class rights are varied, dissentient minorities have special rights to object to the alteration. They must satisfy certain conditions. The dissenters must hold no less than 15% of the issued shares of the class and must not have voted in favour of the resolution (s 633 of the CA 2006). They may then object to the variation within 21 days of consent being given to the resolution. On occasion, objections have been upheld by the court.

Variation of class rights

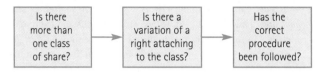

'*Bona fide* for the benefit of the company as a whole'

In addition to the various statutory restrictions considered above, the power to alter a company's articles is subject to the overriding principle that any alteration must be *bona fide* for the benefit of the company as a whole.

In *Allen v Gold Reefs of West Africa Ltd* [1900], the company's articles originally provided:

> ... that the company shall have a first and paramount lien for all debts obligations and liabilities of any member to or towards the company upon all shares (not being fully paid) held by such member ...

▶ ALLEN v GOLD REEFS OF WEST AFRICA LTD [1900]

The company's articles originally provided:

> ... that the company shall have a first and paramount lien for all debts obligations and liabilities of any member to or towards the company upon all shares (not being fully paid) held by such member ...

The alteration proposed was to delete the words 'not being fully paid' to provide the company with a lien over any shares of a member where a debt was due from that member. The alteration was challenged. Lindley MR said as follows:

> Wide, however, as the language of s 50 is [now s 21 of the CA 2006], the power conferred by it must, like all other powers, be

---

> exercised subject to those general principles of law and equity
> which are applicable to all powers conferred on majorities and
> enabling them to bind minorities' stock. It must be exercised,
> not only in the manner required by law, but also *bona fide* for
> the benefit of the company as a whole, and it must not be
> exceeded. These conditions are always implied, and are seldom,
> if ever, expressed. But, if they are complied with, I can discover
> no grounds for judicially putting any other restrictions on the
> power conferred by the section and those contained in it.

In the instant case, the Court of Appeal held that the power had
been exercised *bona fide*.

The case emphasises that if the company's articles are changed it
cannot be for a small group but the interests of the company as a
whole must be considered.

The alteration proposed was to delete the words 'not being fully paid' to provide
the company with a lien over any shares of a member where a debt was
due from that member. The alteration was challenged. Lindley MR said as
follows:

> Wide, however, as the language of s 50 is [now s 21 of the CA 2006],
> the power conferred by it must, like all other powers, be exercised
> subject to those general principles of law and equity which are appli-
> cable to all powers conferred on majorities and enabling them to
> bind minorities' stock. It must be exercised, not only in the manner
> required by law, but also *bona fide* for the benefit of the company as
> a whole, and it must not be exceeded. These conditions are always
> implied, and are seldom, if ever, expressed. But, if they are complied
> with, I can discover no grounds for judicially putting any other
> restrictions on the power conferred by the section and those
> contained in it.

In the instant case, the Court of Appeal held that the power had been exercised
bona fide.

Much of the case law in this area centres upon a discussion as to how one determines whether the alteration is for the benefit of the company as a whole. In *Greenhalgh v Arderne Cinemas Ltd* [1951], it was proposed to delete a preemption provision in the company's articles. The majority shareholder, Mr Mallard, was prompted not by what was in the company's best interests but seemingly out of malice towards a minority shareholder. Lord Evershed MR in the Court of Appeal said:

> Certain principles, I think, can be safely stated as emerging from those authorities. In the first place, I think it is now plain that 'bona fide for the benefit of the company as a whole' is not two things but one thing. It means that the shareholder must proceed upon what in his honest opinion is for the benefit of the company as a whole. The second thing is that the phrase, 'the company as a whole', does not (at any rate in such a case as the present) mean the company as a commercial entity, distinct from the corporators: it means the corporators as a general body. That is to say, the case may be taken of an individual hypothetical member and it may be asked whether what is proposed, is, in the honest opinion of those who voted in its favour, for that person's benefit.

In this case, the Court of Appeal held that the alteration was valid.

Difficulties remain in deciding what is for the benefit of the individual hypothetical member. Hardship to a minority would not automatically invalidate the alteration in question. In *Sidebottom v Kershaw, Leese and Co Ltd* [1920], the Court of Appeal upheld an alteration which permitted the compulsory acquisition of the shares of a minority who was competing with the business of the company. It was held that an alteration permitting such an acquisition was valid even though it was carried out specifically against a particular member. This decision should be contrasted with *Brown v British Abrasive Wheel Co* [1919]. In this case, a 98 per cent majority shareholder wished to insert a provision in the articles requiring the minority who were not prepared to invest further capital in the company to sell their shares as a condition of the majority's subscribing further capital. This alteration was held invalid. In this case the power could not be used by the majority against the minority.

It is extremely rare for the courts to uphold an objection to an alteration of a company's articles on the grounds that it is not *bona fide* for the benefit of the company as a whole.

Sections 994–996 of the CA 2006 do provide a possible remedy for a minority shareholder or indeed any shareholder who has been unfairly prejudiced in the conduct of a company's affairs by the use of voting powers. The courts have also sometimes been willing to act to protect minority shareholders from the oppressive use of majority voting power. This was the case in *Clemens v Clemens Bros Ltd* [1976] and *Estmanco (Kilner House) Ltd v Greater London Council* [1982] as well as in the unreported case *Pennell Securities Ltd v Venida Investments Ltd* [1974].

A provision in the company's articles that an article (or articles) is (or are) unalterable is ineffective (see *Peters' American Delicacy Co Ltd v Heath* [1939]).

It should be re-emphasised that an alteration of the articles cannot be injuncted merely because it results in a breach of contract. The remedy will be in damages (see *Southern Foundries (1926) Ltd v Shirlaw* [1940]).

Lastly, a technique that can be used to prevent a resolution to alter the company's articles being passed is an agreement between the members themselves that they will not vote for such a resolution. This type of agreement was held to be enforceable in *Russell v Northern Development Bank Corp Ltd* [1992]. Of course, the company cannot be a party to such an agreement and new members who were not parties to the agreement would not be bound by it.

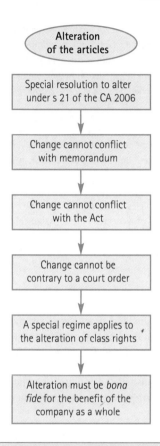

Issues involving alteration of the company's articles often feature on the examination paper. Keep an eye open for variation of class rights and remember, it is not always obvious that the company has more than one class of share.

THE MEMBERSHIP CONTRACT

Section 14 of the CA 1985 was subject to criticism that it lacked clarity. The scope of the provision was reviewed by the Law Commission (Law Commission

Report No 426) in which the Law Commission suggested that s 14 should be viewed as a type of contract which is there to protect the rights of the shareholders. Section 33 CA 2006 continues the 'membership' contract but it is as yet unclear how far s 33 will be applied. However, the Law Commission did also recommend that there should be some form of dispute resolution contained in the articles.

The court has no jurisdiction to rectify the company's articles even though they do not represent the intention of those signing them. This was the *ratio* in *Scott v Frank F Scott (London) Ltd* [1940]. In that case, it was contended by the defendants that the plaintiff was obliged to offer the shares of her deceased husband to them as the other shareholders of the company. It was argued on their behalf that the articles of association should be rectified so as to provide that all ordinary shares of a deceased member should be offered by his executors or administrators to the principal shareholders of the company. It was held that rectification has no part to play in relation to the membership contract. Luxmoore LJ said:

> It seems to us that there is no room in the case of a company incorporated under the appropriate statute or statutes for the application to either the memorandum or articles of association of the principles upon which a Court of Equity permits rectification of documents whether inter partes or not. The memorandum and articles of association of any company which it is proposed to incorporate must be signed by the requisite number of persons who desire its incorporation and must comply with the statutory requirements in respect of registration.

In this respect, the contract is quite different from a normal contract. However, if the understanding of the members differs materially from the constitutional arrangements of the company, this may be a basis for winding the company up on the just and equitable ground under s 122(1)(g) of the IA 1986. In the New Zealand case of *Re North End Motels (Huntly) Ltd* [1976], a retired farmer subscribed for half of the shares in a company on the basis that he would have a say in running the company. He found that he was in a minority on the board of directors and effectively had no say in running the company. He successfully petitioned to wind the company up on the just and equitable ground.

It was formerly the case that a member of a company could not sue for damages for breach of his membership contract while remaining a member of the company. This was a somewhat unusual feature of the membership contract of a company. A member was limited to the remedy of an injunction or a declaration. This was the rule in *Houldsworth v City of Glasgow Bank* [1880]. However, s 655 of the CA 2006 provides:

> ... a person is not debarred from obtaining damages or other compensation from a company by reason only of his holding or having held shares in the company or any right to apply or subscribe for shares or to be included in the company's register in respect of shares.

The s 14 contract was alterable by special resolution in most situations (see above). This therefore means that the terms of the s 14 contract are alterable. The s 14 contract is, of course, also subject to the provisions of CA 2006 and other legislation.

It appears that s 33 of the CA 2006 may not resolve some of the problems identified by the Law Commission so it is worthwhile to look to the common law to fill in the gaps. The section has been interpreted in some cases as only creating rights and duties in respect of membership (or *qua* member). In the leading case of *Hickman v Kent or Romney Marsh Sheep Breeders' Association* [1915], there was an obligation to submit membership disputes to arbitration under Art 49 of the company's articles of association. In this situation, Astbury J said:

> ... in the present case, the plaintiff's action is, in substance, to enforce his rights as a member under the 49 articles against the association. Article 49 is a general article applying to all the members as such, and, apart from technicalities, it would seem reasonable that the plaintiff will not be allowed in the absence of any evidence filed by him to proceed with an action to enforce his rights under the articles, seeing that the action is a breach of his obligation under Art 49 to submit his dispute with the association to arbitration.

The High Court decision has been accepted in later cases. It was accepted in *Beattie v E and F Beattie* [1938] by the Court of Appeal where a member, who was sued in his capacity as a director rather than as a member, was held not to be entitled to rely on the statutory contract to refer a dispute to arbitration. If this interpretation of the section in *Hickman* and *Beattie* is correct then the contract can only be invoked in respect of membership rights and obligations and not, for example, in disputes between officers and the company. Thus, in *Eley v Positive Government Security Life Assurance Co* [1876], the articles provided that Eley should be solicitor to the company. He was a member of the company but was unable to enforce the article in his capacity as company solicitor.

In *Pender v Lushington* [1877], a member was able to restrain a company from acting on the basis that he could not demand a poll of the members and, in *Wood v Odessa Waterworks Company* [1889], a member was able to enforce the terms of the articles to have a dividend paid in cash. In both cases, the member was acting *qua* member.

ACADEMIC VIEWS

▢ Professor Gower (*Principles of Modern Company Law*) espouses the view that [s 33 of the CA 2006] can only be utilised *qua* member:

The decisions have constantly confirmed that the section confers contractual effect on a provision in the articles only in so far as it affords rights or imposes obligations on a member qua member.

▢ A contrary view is put forward in an article in the *Cambridge Law Journal* by Lord Wedderburn in 'Shareholders' rights and the rule in *Foss v Harbottle* [1957] CLJ 194'. In this article, Lord Wedderburn argues that the decision in *Quin and Axtens v Salmon* [1909], permitting a member to obtain an injunction restraining the company from concluding agreements entered into in breach of the company's articles, showed that the member was able to enforce his rights as a director.

The cases are difficult to reconcile.

▢ In the *Modern Law Review* ((1972) 35 MLR 362), GD Goldberg argues that a member has a contractual right to have the affairs of the company conducted by the particular organ of the company specified in the act or the company's constitution. GN Prentice, by contrast, argues that a member *qua* member can sue the company where the particular provision affects the power of the company to function ((1980) 1 Co Law 179). It is probably impossible to square the decided cases with any one view.

- R Gregory probably comes close to the truth when he argues ((1981) 44 MLR 526) that the older case law is confused and inconsistent.

- R Drury ([1986] CLJ 219) takes a view that is similar to that of Lord Wedderburn.

It has been noted that the membership contract is also enforceable between members *inter se*. This was the *ratio* of the decision in *Rayfield v Hands* [1960]. In *London Sack and Bag Ltd v Dixon and Lugton* [1943], the court refused to enforce a provision in the company's constitution between two members as it did not concern them as members. This returns us to the debate between Professor Gower and Lord Wedderburn.

On occasion, the company's memorandum and articles may form the basis of a separate contract. This happened in *Re New British Iron Co ex p Beckwith* [1898] where directors of the company were able to imply a contract on the same terms as the articles when suing for their fees.

However, if this is the case, the contract incorporating the terms of the company's articles may well be determined to be on alterable terms since the articles are freely alterable. Thus, in *Swabey v Port Darwin Gold Mining Co* [1889], the court took the view that the company could alter its articles and so affect the terms of the contract for the future.

Where there is a contract on the same terms as the articles, there may be an implied term that the contract is fixed at a particular date so that the contract is not freely alterable (see *Southern Foundries (1926) Ltd v Shirlaw* [1940]).

It may, therefore, be seen how the membership contract differs from an orthodox type of contract. Examiners often delight in such distinctions. This area lends itself to essay questions but it may also feature as part of a problem question. You should be familiar with the law in the area under the CA 2006.

You should now be confident that you would be able to tick all of the boxes on the checklist at the beginning of this chapter. To check your knowledge of The company's constitution why not visit the companion website and take the Multiple Choice Question test. Check your understanding of the terms and vocabulary used in this chapter with the flashcard glossary.

Capital

3

INTRODUCTION

The word 'capital' is used in this context as the money and assets raised by the company by the issue of shares. Likely examination areas are reviewed in depth in this chapter, beginning with the legal issues connected with the issue of shares.

PROMOTERS

Promoters, pre-incorporation contracts, prospectuses and listing particulars are favourite examination topics. Very often, they are linked together so that, in a problem question, two or more of these areas may be combined.

DEFINITION OF A PROMOTER

There is no satisfactory definition of a promoter. There is no definition in any of the relevant statutes. It is wise, however, to be familiar with some of the *dicta* in the cases as questions often revolve around the question of whether a particular individual in a problem is a promoter or not. In *Twycross v Grant* [1877], Cockburn CJ defined a company promoter as a person who 'undertakes to form a company with reference to a given project and to set it going and who takes the necessary steps to accomplish that purpose'. In *Emma Silver Mining Co v Grant* [1879], Lord Lindley said that the term had 'no very definite meaning'. The question of whether a person is a promoter or not is a question of fact.

> ### ❱ TWYCROSS v GRANT [1877]
>
> Cockburn CJ defined a company promoter as a person who 'undertakes to form a company with reference to a given project and to set it going and who takes the necessary steps to accomplish that purpose'. This is the best and most widely accepted attempt to define a promoter.

DUTIES OF A PROMOTER

Inevitably, if questions involve promoters there will be an issue relating to the duties of the promoters. Promoters owe fiduciary duties to the company they are promoting. The duties are very similar to those owed by directors to their company and by trustees to their trust.

A promoter must not, therefore, make a profit out of the promotion unless it is disclosed to the company and unless the company agrees to his retention of the profits. The promoter should disclose any profits that he is making from the promotion either to an independent board of directors, as discussed in *Erlanger v New Sombrero Phosphate Co Ltd* [1878], or, alternatively, to all of the shareholders, actual and potential, as in *Salomon v Salomon & Co Ltd* [1897].

The duty of disclosure is a duty to disclose all profits, whether direct or indirect. Thus, in *Gluckstein v Barnes* [1900], where the promoter failed to disclose a profit that he had made by buying up a mortgage at a discount, he was held liable to disgorge that profit back to the company.

Another aspect of the fiduciary duties of promoters is that if a promoter acquires property during a promotion period, he holds that property on trust for the company. There appears to be no English case which has this as the *ratio decidendi*. However, there are *dicta* in *Ladywell Mining Co v Brookes* [1887] to that effect.

Where full disclosure of any profits has not been made, various remedies are open to the company in the normal run of events. First, the company may seek to rescind the contract with the promoter. The remedy of rescission is, however, subject to the normal bars to that remedy. Thus, there can be no rescission if there has been affirmation of the contract, if third party rights have intervened or if restitution of the property is no longer possible. A second possible remedy is to recover the profit from the promoter rather than to rescind the contract. These two remedies are alternatives. Thus, in *Gluckstein v Barnes* [1900], recovery of the indirect profit was granted to the company. The remedy of disgorgement is not available where the promoter has acquired the property in a pre-promotion period. In such a situation, not all of the profit that has accrued is rightly the company's, even where there has been no disclosure. The courts will not intervene in a situation such as this to try to apportion the profits. Instead, it seems that in such a situation the only remedy that is available is that of rescission (see *Re Cape Breton Co* [1885], *Cavendish Bentinck v Fenn* [1887] and *Ladywell Mining Co v Brookes* [1887]).

On occasion, it may be that neither of these remedies is available. This would be the case, for example, if the property was acquired pre-promotion so that some of the profit is attributable to a pre-promotion period and if the remedy of rescission is blocked for one of the reasons set out above.

In one case, the remedy of damages was made available to the company. The company was awarded the difference between the market price and the contract price where the company paid over the odds for the property. The property in question was the purchase of two music halls (*Re Leeds and Hanley Theatres of Varieties* [1902]).

Particular problems arise in relation to the remuneration of promoters. There can be no obligation in contract between the promoter and the company. The company is not in existence and therefore cannot have entered into any contract with the promoter (see *Re National MotorMail Coach Co Ltd (Clinton's Claim)* [1908]).

A promoter may be disqualified from acting as a director, liquidator, administrative receiver or administrator, or being otherwise involved in the business. Under the Company Directors Disqualification Act 1986, an order may be made against any person. All disqualifications are subject to this Act. The disqualification may, in extreme cases, last for up to 15 years. As an alternative to disqualification proceedings, the Act provides for a person to give an undertaking to the Secretary of State to the same effect.

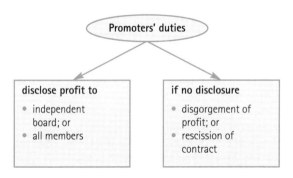

PRE-INCORPORATION CONTRACTS

As has been mentioned, an area that is often coupled with promoters is that of pre-incorporation contracts. This is the situation where a person enters into a contract on behalf of an unformed company.

POSITION UNDER STATUTE

Section 51 of the Companies Act (CA) 2006 provides:

> . . . a contract which purports to be made by or on behalf of a company at a time when the company has not been formed, has effect, subject to any agreement to the contrary, as one made with the person purporting to act for the company or as agent for it, and he is personally liable on that contract accordingly.

In *Phonogram Ltd v Lane* [1982], the court had to consider the effect of this section where a company called Fragile Management Ltd was in the process of being incorporated. The company was to manage a pop group called Cheap, Mean and Nasty. The defendant was the manager of the pop group. He agreed with the claimant that the claimant would supply finance. He signed an agreement undertaking to repay the monies that had been advanced on behalf of Fragile Management Ltd if the contract was not completed before a certain date. Subsequently, the claimant sued the defendant for the money that had been advanced. The defendant argued that he was not personally liable on the agreement. It was suggested on his behalf that the contract was not 'purported' to be made by the company as it was known that the company was not in existence. Indeed it was known by both parties that the company had not yet been formed. However, Lord Denning MR took the view that a contract can purport to be made on behalf of a company, even though the company is known by both parties to the agreement not to have been formed. The section could only be excluded by express contrary agreement. The other members of the Court of Appeal shared this view.

For other examples of the application of s 51 of the CA 2006, see *Oshkosh B'Gosh v Dan Marbel Inc* [1989]; *Badgerhill Properties Ltd v Cottrell* [1991]; *Cotronic (UK) Ltd v Dezonie* [1991]. In *Braymist Ltd v Wise Finance Co Ltd* [2001] it was held that s 51of the CA 2006 could be relied on by a promoter in order to *enforce* a pre-incorporation contract.

PROSPECTUSES AND LISTING PARTICULARS

It is most unusual for examiners to require students to know the detailed rules relating to the content of listing particulars and prospectuses. In relation to prospectuses (which are those documents prepared by companies offering

49

shares or debentures to the public which are not listed on the official list of the Stock Exchange), the rules are set out in the Public Offers of Securities Regulations 1995.

In relation to listing particulars (the document produced by companies that are quoted on the official list of the Stock Exchange which are offering shares or debentures to the public), the detailed rules are set out in the Listing Rules. Section 80 of the Financial Services and Markets Act (FSMA) 2000 provides in relation to listing particulars that:

> ... in addition to the information specified by listing rules or required by the competent authority [the Financial Services Authority] as a condition of the admission of any securities to the official list, any listing particulars submitted to the competent authority ... shall contain all such information as investors and their professional advisers would reasonably require, and reasonably expect to find there, for the purpose of making an informed assessment of:
>
> (a) the assets and liabilities, financial position, profits and losses, and prospects of the issue of the securities; and
> (b) the rights attaching to those securities.

CIVIL LIABILITIES

Most questions involving a consideration of prospectuses or listing particulars require an assessment of the remedies that may be available to a misled investor.

The rules for the two types of documents are similar. The statutory remedy for those who suffer loss as a result of misleading listing particulars is set out in s 90 of the FSMA 2000. Any investor who purchases securities and suffers loss as a result of misleading listing particulars is eligible for compensation, unless one of the defences applies.

Where a misleading prospectus is issued, regs 13 to 15 of the Public Offers of Securities Regulations 1995 provide an identical remedy.

There are other remedies available to those subscribing for, or purchasing, shares as a result of misleading listing particulars or prospectuses. It makes no difference, however, whether the purchaser or subscriber has relied upon either a prospectus or listing particulars in this regard.

Thus, the remedy of rescission may be available where a person subscribes for shares on the basis of misleading listing particulars or a misleading prospectus. The usual bars to rescission will apply. Thus, if there has been affirmation, or the intervention of third party rights, or if restitution is not possible, rescission will not be available. Obviously, the remedy of rescission is only available to a subscriber against the company, the other contracting party.

If the claimant has been induced to purchase shares or debentures on the basis of a misleading prospectus or misleading listing particulars, he may have a remedy for the misrepresentation under statute. It has already been seen that he may seek rescission. In addition, damages may be available in lieu of rescission: see s 2(2) of the Misrepresentation Act 1967. Damages may also be available under s 2(1) of the Misrepresentation Act 1967.

Section 2(1) of the Misrepresentation Act 1967 provides that damages may be awarded where loss has occurred through a misrepresentation, unless the representor can prove that he had reasonable grounds to believe, and did believe, up to the time the contract was made that the facts represented were true. The section only applies if the representor is a party to the contract. It therefore means that the remedy is only available to a subscriber for shares. The measure of damages under s 2(1) of the Misrepresentation Act 1967 is the same as for the tort of deceit (*Royscot Trust Ltd v Rogerson* [1991]).

A remedy may be available in tort. In relation to tortious remedies, it is conceivable that the remedy may be available both to a subscriber purchasing shares or debentures directly from the company and to a purchaser on the open market who buys from another person after relying upon the content of the prospectus or listing particulars. The claimant may seek to obtain damages in the tort of deceit. He would need to show that there is a statement of fact which is fraudulent or which is made recklessly as to its truth. In *Derry v Peek* [1889], a prospectus was issued by a tramway company. The company was empowered to use horse-drawn trams in Plymouth. The prospectus stated that the company was empowered to use steam-driven vehicles. This was not the case. Permission had been sought from the Board of Trade to use steam driven trams but was refused. It was held that since the directors honestly believed the statement to be true, they were not liable for fraud. An action in the tort of deceit may be brought against the company itself or against the directors. Since the remedy in contract is available against the company itself, it is not likely to be used by a subscriber for shares. It may, however, be used where a purchaser of shares on the open market wishes to bring an action in tort where he cannot bring one in contract. He would need to demonstrate that the prospectus or listing particulars are designed to encourage purchases of shares on the open market (see *Andrews v Mockford* [1896]). In this case, the Court of Appeal considered that the prospectus was designed to induce application both for the allotment of shares from the public and for the purchase of shares in the open market.

An action may also lie in damages for the tort of negligent misstatement in accordance with the principles of *Hedley Byrne v Heller* [1963]. In such an instance, it must be shown that the company owed a duty of care to the investor. It will be easier to demonstrate negligence as opposed to deceit, but it will be necessary to show that a 'special relationship' exists.

These are the most important matters to consider in relation to prospectuses and listing particulars so far as the examination is concerned, but you should also familiarise yourself with the provisions in relation to criminal liability.

CRIMINAL LIABILITY

If a person involved in carrying on an investment business issues false listing particulars or a false prospectus, he will be guilty of an offence in certain situations under s 397 of the FSMA 2000. If such a person makes a statement, promise or forecast which he knows to be misleading, false or deceptive, or dishonestly conceals any material facts or recklessly makes (dishonestly or otherwise) a statement, promise or forecast which is misleading, false or deceptive, if it is for the purpose of inducing another to enter into any investment agreement, he is guilty of an offence. The section also makes it an offence to do any act or engage in conduct creating a false or misleading impression as to the market in or value of any investment if it is done to induce another to acquire, dispose of, subscribe for or underwrite those investments or to refrain from doing so or to exercise or refrain from exercising any rights conferred by those investments. It is a defence if the person concerned can prove that he reasonably believed that his act or conduct would not create an impression that was false or misleading. The maximum penalty is seven years' imprisonment.

Under s 98 of the FSMA 2000 it is an offence to publish an advertisement of securities without the approval of 'the competent authority'. An authorised person under the Act who contravenes the section is liable to disciplinary action whereas an unauthorised person is liable to up to two years' imprisonment and/ or a fine on indictment. This applies to listing particulars and to prospectuses (s 86 of the FSMA 2000).

A copy of listing particulars must be deposited with the registrar of companies. Failure to do so is an offence under s 83 of the FSMA 2000 punishable on indictment by a fine. This also applies to prospectuses (s 86 of the FSMA 2000).

It is an offence for a private company to issue an advertisement offering its securities to the public (s 755 of the CA 2006).

Section 400(1) of the FSMA 2000 provides that where an offence is committed by a company and is proved to have been committed with the consent or connivance of, or to be attributable to, any neglect on the part of any director, manager, secretary or other similar officer of the company, or any person who is purporting to act in any such capacity, or a controller of the company, he as well as the body corporate shall be guilty of that offence and liable to be proceeded against and punished accordingly.

Section 19 of the Theft Act 1968 provides that an officer or person purporting to act as such with the intention of deceiving members or creditors of a company who publishes a statement or account which he knows is, or may be, misleading is guilty of an offence. This carries a maximum sentence of seven years' imprisonment.

Summary of remedies for misleading prospectuses and listing particulars

■ **Statute**
Any investor who has suffered loss:
 − listing particulars: s 90 of the FSMA 2000
 − prospectus: Public Offers of Securities Regulations 1995 (regs 13–15)

■ **Contract (subscribers only):**
 − rescission
 − breach of contract
 − Misrepresentation Act 1967

53

■ **Tort**

Potentially any investor if the prospectus or listing particulars are designed to encourage market purchases:

— fraud
— negligent misstatement

SHARES

Shares were defined in *Borland's Trustee v Steel Bros & Co Ltd* [1901] by Farwell J as 'the interest of the shareholder in the company measured by a sum of money, for the purpose of liability in the first place, and of interest in the second, but also consisting of a series of mutual covenants entered into by all the shareholders inter se' [in accordance with what is now s 33 of the CA 2006].

The most usual type of share is the ordinary share. However, there may be different classes of shares which entitle the shareholders to different rights such as dividends, repayment of capital or rights to vote. Generally a share will give a right to a dividend, a right to vote at general meetings, a right to transfer the share in accordance with the articles, any rights of membership that attach to that class of share, the obligation to pay for the share and the right to receive assets if the company goes into liquidation.

Other types of shares include preference shares, which entitle the holder to receive a fixed return on the shares, and redeemable preference shares, which are similar to preference shares but may be redeemed at the option of the company on a set date.

One common area that may form part of a problem question on shares is that of pre-emption rights. If a shareholder wishes to sell their shares then existing shareholders have the right to be offered those shares before they are offered for general share (*Greehalgh v Mallard* [1943]).

RULES RELATING TO PAYMENT FOR SHARES

The following matters should be checked where shares are to be issued by a public or a private company:

▨ Does the company have sufficient authorised share capital for the issue? This may be checked by looking at the company's memorandum. If necessary, the authorised capital may be increased: see s 617 of the CA 2006.

▨ Do the directors have authority to allot the shares? See s 549 of the CA 2006. However, a private company may pass an elective resolution that s 549 of the CA 2006 is not to apply to that company, since, normally, authority under s 551 of the CA 2006 can only last for a maximum period of five years, unless renewed.

▨ Do pre-emption rights apply? Section 561 of the CA 2006 makes statutory provision for pre-emption on second and subsequent issues of shares. This may be excluded by a private company in its constitution (see s 567 of the CA 2006).

It may be excluded by both public and private companies by special resolution (see s 571 of the CA 2006).

▨ The rules for payment for shares are based upon the Second EC Directive on Company Law. They are incorporated into the CA 2006.

Section 582(1) and (3) of the CA 2006 requires that shares should be paid up in money or money's worth.

Section 585(1) of the CA 2006 provides that a public company cannot accept an undertaking from a person to do work or perform services for shares.

Section 580 of the CA 2006 requires that shares cannot be issued at a discount. This applies to both public and private companies. There are, however, exceptions to this principle:

● Shares may be issued to underwriters at a discount of up to 10 per cent (s 553 of the CA 2006).

● Shares may be issued in exchange for services that happen to be overvalued in a private company. Shares may not be issued in exchange for services in a public company.

● Shares may be issued in exchange for property which is overvalued in a private company. In a public company, there is a need for an independent expert valuation of the property concerned (s 593 of the CA 2006).

In a public company, shares must be paid up to at least one quarter of their nominal value plus the whole of any premium (s 586 of the CA 2006).

A public company cannot issue shares in exchange for a noncash consideration which may be transferred more than five years from the date of allotment (s 587(1) of the CA 2006).

Where shares are issued at a premium (that is, above their nominal value) in either a private or a public company, the whole of the premium is placed in a share premium account. This is treated as if it were ordinary share capital for most purposes. It cannot be used to pay up a dividend. However, it may be used to pay up a bonus issue of shares (s 610 of the CA 2006).

RULES RELATING TO THE MAINTENANCE OF CAPITAL

The common law rule was that it was illegal for a company to acquire its own shares. Below, you will find a summary of the overall purpose of these rules, as explained by Lord Watson in *Trevor v Whitworth* [1877]:

> The capital may, no doubt, be diminished by expenditure upon and reasonably incidental to all the objects specified. A part of it may be lost in carrying on the business operations authorised. Of this, all persons trusting the company are aware, and take the risk. But I think [those dealing with the company] have a right to rely, and were intended by the legislature to have a right to rely, on the capital remaining undiminished by any expenditure outside these limits, or by the return of any part of it to the shareholders.

The statutory rules on the maintenance of capital can be outlined as follows:

- Companies are prohibited from purchasing their own shares, subject to certain exceptions (s 658(1) of the CA 2006).

- Section 684(1) of the CA 2006 allows companies to issue redeemable shares, that is, shares which are issued on terms that they will be 'bought back' by the company at a future date (*Barclays Bank plc v British and Commonwealth Holdings plc* [1996]).

- Section 690(1) of the CA 2006 allows companies to purchase their own shares, even though not issued as redeemable shares, subject to certain restrictions.

▣ Public companies can only redeem or purchase their own shares out of profits or out of the proceeds of a fresh issue of shares. Private companies may purchase out of capital subject to certain safeguards (s 709(1) of the CA 2006).

Public companies are generally prohibited from providing financial assistance towards the purchase of their own shares (s 678(1) of the CA 2006) (see *Brady v Brady* [1989]; *Chaston v SWP Group plc* [2002]). There are unconditional exceptions to this principle set out in s 681 of the CA 2006:

(a) a distribution of the company's assets by way of a dividend lawfully made, or a distribution in the course of a company's winding up;
(b) an allotment of bonus shares;
(c) a reduction of capital;
(d) a redemption of shares;
(e) anything done in pursuance of an order of the court sanctioning compromise or arrangement with members or creditors;
(f) anything done under an arrangement made in pursuance of s 110 of the Insolvency Act 1986;
(g) anything done under an arrangement made between a company and its creditors that is binding on the creditors by virtue of Part 1 of the Insolvency Act 1986.

There are further conditional exceptions for public companies in s 682 of the CA 2006.

▣ Companies may reduce their capital by passing a special resolution to this effect and obtaining the consent of the court to the reduction (s 641(1) of the CA 2006).

▣ If a public company suffers a serious loss of capital (net assets worth half or less of called up share capital), then a general meeting is required to be called to alert the shareholders within 28 days of discovering that the loss of capital has occurred. The meeting should take place within 56 days (s 656 of the CA 2006).

THE PAYMENT OF DIVIDENDS

Under s 820 the rules of the CA 2006 (from 2008) apply to 'every description of a company's assets to its members, whether in cash or otherwise'.

Section 830(2) of the CA 2006 provides that distributions can only be made out of accumulated, realised profits less accumulated, realised losses.

Section 831 of the CA 2006 applies to public companies. It requires the public company to maintain the capital side of its account in addition to having available profits. Therefore, if the company's net assets are worth less than the subscribed share capital plus undistributable reserves at the end of the trading period, that shortfall must first be made good out of distributable profits before a dividend can be paid.

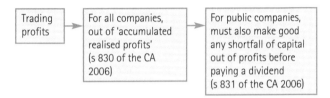

If a dividend is wrongly paid, a member may be liable to repay it under s 847 of the CA 2006.

Directors who are responsible for unlawful distributions can be held liable for breach of duty (see *Flitcroft's Case* [1882]; *Bairstow v Queens' Moat Houses plc* [2002]).

If the directors have relied upon the auditors in recommending a dividend, then the auditors may be liable (see *Dovey v Cory* [1901]).

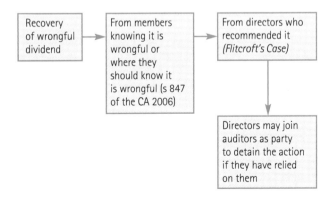

An interesting case arose in *Progress Property Co Ltd v Moorgarth Group Ltd*
[2010] SC. This concerned the issue of whether the sale of the whole of the
issued share capital of a company at what was argued to be an undervalue and
thus was an unlawful distribution. It was suggested that the relevant sections
were 829 and 830 CA 2006 but the

> common law rule devised for the protection of the creditors of a
> company is well settled: a distribution of a company's assets to a
> shareholder, except in accordance with specific statutory procedures,
> such as a winding up of the company, is a return of capital, which is
> unlawful and *ultra vires* the company.

To determine what the true nature of the transaction was the court had to investigate of all the relevant facts, which sometimes include the state of mind of the
human beings involved. In the case it was found to be a genuine commercial sale.

REFORM OF FINANCIAL REGULATION

In June 2011 a White Paper was published which outlined the proposed new
structure of financial regulation. This is expected to be in place by the end of
2012 or early 2013 so students should be aware that amendments to the system
of financial regulation are forthcoming. The principal aim of the review is to
'fundamentally strengthen the system by promoting the role of judgement and
expertise'. This will be done by the creation of three new bodies to regulate
different parts of the financial system. These bodies are planned to be the
Financial Policy Committee (FPC), the Prudential Regulation Authority (PRA) and
the Financial Conduct Authority (FCA). One consequence of the establishment
of these bodies will be the abolition of the Financial Services Authority (FSA).
Most of its current powers will be exercised by the FCA. It was also announced
that the Financial Services and Markets Act (FSMA) 2000 would be amended
rather than repealed.

> You should now be confident that you would be able to tick all of the
> boxes on the checklist at the beginning of this chapter. To check your
> knowledge of Capital why not visit the companion website and take the
> Multiple Choice Question test. Check your understanding of the terms
> and vocabulary used in this chapter with the flashcard glossary.

4

The management of the company

INTRODUCTION

The material contained in this chapter is highly likely to form at least one question on any company law examination paper, particularly in light of the changes introduced under the Companies Act 2006. We begin by looking at the law surrounding the removal of directors before going on to examine the topic of directors' duties. Lastly, the main points in relation to the company secretary and auditors are noted.

REMOVAL OF DIRECTORS

The key issue which is often examinable – sometimes in essay form and sometimes as part of a problem question – concerns the removal of directors.

Section 168(1) of the Companies Act (CA) 2006 provides that a director may be removed from the board of directors by ordinary resolution in general meeting notwithstanding anything contained in his employment contract. This is a change from the provisions of s 303 of the CA 1985. Although this looks to be a powerful weapon for the shareholders, it is subject to qualifications. First, s 168(5) of CA 2006 preserves the right of a director dismissed under s 168 to damages for any breach of contract unless s 188 of the CA 2006 can be used. Second, the case of *Bushell v Faith* [1970] outlines the use of provisions in the company's constitution. In this case, a small private company concerned with the management of a block of flats in Southgate, North London was at the centre of the dispute. The shares were held by two sisters and a brother. The two sisters wished to remove the brother from the board of directors. Since the shares were held equally, on the face of it, this should present no problem. However, a provision in the company's articles of association stated that on a resolution to remove a director from office, his shares would carry three votes each. If this were valid, it would have the effect of entrenching the brother and preventing his removal. Nor would it be possible to alter the company's articles as this would require a special resolution. The House of Lords held by a majority of four to one that the provision was valid. The brother was therefore protected from removal. The scope of *Bushell v Faith* is probably limited following the amendment of the legislation.

▶ BUSHELL v FAITH [1970]

The shares in a small private company were held by two sisters and a brother. The two sisters wished to remove the brother from the board of directors. Since the shares were held equally, on the face of it, this should present no problem. However, a provision in the company's articles of association stated that on a resolution to remove a director from office, his shares would carry three votes each. If this were valid, it would have the effect of entrenching the brother and preventing his removal. Nor would it be possible to alter the company's articles as this would require a special resolution.

The House of Lords held by a majority of four to one that the provision was valid. The brother was therefore protected from removal.

The case illustrates the importance of weighted voting clauses but its scope is probably limited following the amendment of s 168 CA 2006.

In the same way, a provision in the company's constitution requiring a particular quorum at a meeting to remove a director would probably also be doubted (see *Re BML Group Ltd* [1994], for example, in respect of the attendance of the shareholder whose directorship was under threat).

Section 188(1) of the CA 2006 does, however, provide that a director cannot have a service agreement for a period of more than two years unless the term is first approved by a resolution of the company in general meeting. (This is a reduction from the five years allowed under s 319 of CA 1985). This provision, therefore, counteracts the possibility of a director having a long service agreement at high remuneration and then suing for compensation if removed from the board of directors. It may nevertheless prove expensive for a private company, and indeed sometimes a public company, to remove a director from the board (see *Shindler v Northern Raincoat Co Ltd* [1960]; *Southern Foundries (1926) Ltd v Shirlaw* [1940]). The Listing Rules require boards to report to the shareholders annually with details of any directors' service contract with a notice period of more than one year.

On occasion, a company may place in its constitution a liquidated damages provision which states that if a director is removed from the board he is entitled to a set amount of compensation. Provided that this sum is not a penalty, the director may enforce this provision (see *Taupo Totara Timber Co Ltd v Rowe* [1977]). This was a Privy Council decision on appeal from New Zealand (see below).

That apart, s 215 of the CA 2006 makes it unlawful for a company to give a director of the company any payment by way of compensation for loss of office, without particulars of the proposed payment (including its amount) being disclosed to members of the company and the proposal being approved by the company. However, this does not apply to payment by way of compensation for breach of contract (s 220(1) of the CA 2006). Members can find out about the nature of any director's termination payment by virtue of the disclosure provisions of s 228(1) of the CA 2006. These provisions extend to directors' remuneration generally and, in the case of s 228 of the CA 2006, extend to all the terms of a director's contract of service.

A director may enter into voting agreements with shareholders who may agree to vote as directed by him or to protect his position from removal. Such agreements, provided they are supported by consideration, would be enforceable by mandatory injunction (see *Puddephatt v Leith* [1916]; *Greenwell v Porter* [1902]).

It was formerly the case that, in a quasi-partnership company (such as the company in *Ebrahimi v Westbourne Galleries Ltd* [1973]), where a director was removed from the board, he could petition to wind the company up on the just and equitable ground on the basis that it was contrary to the understanding reached when the company was formed. In *Ebrahimi*, he and Nazar had run a successful partnership business selling carpets and tapestries. The company had been incorporated and had thrived. Later, Nazar's son was introduced to the business and both he and Ebrahimi transferred shares to Nazar's son, George. Discord followed and Nazar and George removed Ebrahimi from the board of directors. They had a majority of the shares and votes. The profits of the business were paid out as directors' salaries rather than dividends. Exclusion from the board therefore hit Ebrahimi in the pocket as well as hurting his pride. He sought and obtained a winding up order under the CA 1948. The House of Lords held unanimously that a winding up order should be granted.

❯ EBRAHIMI v WESTBOURNE GALLERIES LTD [1973]

Ebrahimi and Nazar had run a successful partnership business selling carpets and tapestries. The company had been incorporated and had thrived. Later, Nazar's son was introduced to the business and both he and Ebrahimi transferred shares to Nazar's son. Discord followed. Nazar and his son removed Ebrahimi from the board of directors. They had a majority of the shares and votes. The profits of the business were paid out as directors' salaries rather than dividends. Exclusion from the board therefore hit Ebrahimi in the pocket as well as hurting his pride. He sought and obtained a winding up order under the CA 1948.

The House of Lords held unanimously that a winding up order should be granted.

The case demonstrates that in a quasi-partnership company, where a director was removed from the board, he could petition to wind the company up on the just and equitable ground on the basis that it was contrary to the understanding reached when the company was formed.

Such situations are now unlikely. Section 125(2) of the Insolvency Act (IA) 1986 requires the court, if it is of the opinion that the petitioner is entitled to relief, to decide whether it is just and equitable that the company should be wound up, bearing in mind the possibility of other forms of relief. The court, if it comes to the conclusion that it would be just and equitable that the company should be wound up in the absence of any other remedy, must make a winding up order unless it is of the opinion that the petitioner is acting unreasonably in not pursuing that other remedy. In most situations, it will surely be unreasonable to pursue the winding up remedy where there is a possibility of a successful petition under ss 994–996 of the CA 2006. However, in *Virdi v Abbey Leisure Ltd* [1990], the court did consider that a refusal by the shareholder to accept an offer to buy his shares where he feared that the valuation would be wrong was not unreasonable.

There have been many successful petitions under ss 994–996 of the CA 2006 on the grounds of removal from management. Most of the cases concern quasi-partnership companies. One successful petition was in *Re Bovey Hotel Ventures*

Ltd [1981]. It is unlikely in the case of a public company that a petition on the basis of exclusion from management would be successful (see *Re Blue Arrow plc* [1987]; *Re Astec (BSR) plc* [1998]).

Wherever a director is to be removed under s 168, special notice must be served. Special notice is defined in s 312 of the CA 2006. This is 28 days' notice of the resolution from the person who is proposing the removal. The notice is given by depositing a copy of the resolution at the company's registered office.

The resolution should then be forwarded forthwith to the director concerned. The director may make representations in writing which should then be circulated to every member of the company to whom notice of the meeting is to be sent. If it is not sent for some reason, the representations must be read out at the meeting. An exception to the requirement of circulation or oral presentation is if the representations contain defamatory matter in which case application should be made to the court which will then decide if it is thought appropriate to circulate or for the director to read out the representations.

The director also has a right to speak at the meeting where his removal is proposed in his own defence in addition to the circulation of the representations.

In the absence of anything to the contrary in the articles, a single shareholder cannot give special notice under s 168 of the CA 2006 proposing a resolution to remove a director and requiring the company to circulate all of the members for the obvious reason that this would be very expensive for the company. Instead, the threshold contained in s 314(1) and (4) of the CA 2006 has to be satisfied, that is, members representing not less than a quarter of the total voting rights of all the members or not less than 100 members holding shares on which they have been paid up an average sum per member of not less than £100 have requisitioned the company for such a resolution (see *Pedley v Inland Waterways Association Ltd* [1977]).

Although s 288 of the Companies Act 2006 contains a written resolution procedure where members of a private company agree unanimously on a course of action, this does not apply to the removal of directors. The reason for this is that the director concerned has a right to speak in his own defence, a right which can only be guaranteed by the meeting itself.

It may be seen there is much material here for answering a question on the removal of directors. Since there are many protections for directors, it lends

67

itself to examination questions and students should therefore ensure that they know this area in detail.

Removal of directors – summary

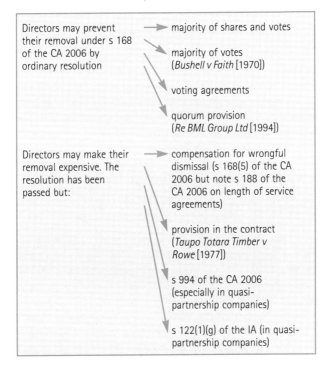

Directors may prevent their removal under s 168 of the CA 2006 by ordinary resolution
→ majority of shares and votes

↘ majority of votes (*Bushell v Faith* [1970])

↘ voting agreements

↘ quorum provision (*Re BML Group Ltd* [1994])

Directors may make their removal expensive. The resolution has been passed but:
→ compensation for wrongful dismissal (s 168(5) of the CA 2006 but note s 188 of the CA 2006 on length of service agreements)

↘ provision in the contract (*Taupo Totara Timber v Rowe* [1977])

↘ s 994 of the CA 2006 (especially in quasi-partnership companies)

↘ s 122(1)(g) of the IA (in quasi-partnership companies)

DIRECTORS' DUTIES

It is inconceivable that an examination paper in company law could be set without touching on the area of directors' duties. A question may take the form of an essay or may be in problem form, possibly involving other areas such as minority shareholder protection. Directors' duties may be conveniently split into two parts: the directors' duty of care and skill and directors' fiduciary duties. The rules have now been codified in the CA 2006 so that the prior caselaw remains important.

Directors owe their duties to the company, which is interpreted as meaning the providers of capital, that is, the company's shareholders. This means the shareholders as a body rather than individual shareholders. Thus, in *Percival v Wright* [1902], certain shareholders approached directors and asked if the directors would purchase their shares. Negotiations took place but the directors failed to mention that a takeover bid had been made for the company. This materially affected the value of the shares. The court held that there had been no breach of duty by the directors. The directors owed their duties to the body of shareholders rather than individual shareholders and premature disclosure of the takeover negotiations could well have amounted to a breach of duty. The decision might have been different if the approach had been made by the directors to the shareholders (see *Briess v Woolley* [1954]) or if there had been a special relationship of trust between the directors and the shareholders, as in *Allen v Hyatt* [1914] and *Coleman v Myers* [1977]. A more recent example, affirming the general position, is *Peskin v Anderson* [2001]. In this case, the directors were held not to owe a duty to former shareholders to inform them of the disposal of a company asset, which resulted in existing members each receiving a windfall of £34,000, as there was no special factual relationship generating a fiduciary obligation, such as a duty of disclosure.

Section 172(1) of the CA 2006 provides that the matters to which the directors of a company are to have regard in the performance of their functions include the interests of the company's employees in general as well as the interests of its members.

The provision might seem to be radical in that it extends the category of persons that directors should take account of to include the providers of labour, but, in fact, the duty is enforceable in the same way as other duties and ultimately is only enforceable by the company. Accordingly, the duty imposed by s 172 of the CA 2006 on the directors of a company is owed by them to the company.

It is perhaps worth noting in passing that s 247 of the CA 2006 permits a company to make payments to its employees on ceasing to trade or a company transferring its business. This was something that was previously *ultra vires* the company if there was no business that was capable of being benefited (see *Parke v Daily News Ltd* [1962]).

Sometimes, *dicta* in the cases indicate other duties that may be owed by directors. On occasion, judges may make reference to a duty being owed to creditors (see *Winkworth v Edward Baron Developments Ltd* [1986]), but it appears that the true position is that directors do not owe duties directly to creditors. Any obligation requiring the directors to consider the interests of creditors is owed to the company alone and only when the company is insolvent (see *Kuwait Asia Bank EC v National Mutual Life Nominees Ltd* [1991]; *Liquidator of West Mercia Safetywear Ltd v Dodd* [1988]; *Yukong Lines Ltd of Korea v Rendsburg Investments Corp of Liberia* [1998]). Creditors are protected by provisions contained in the Insolvency Act (IA) 1986 and elsewhere.

THE DUTY OF CARE AND SKILL

Under the Companies Act 2006 the general duties of directors have been placed on a statutory basis. These can be found in s 170 of the CA 2006. Section 170(3) states that

> . . . the general duties are based on certain common law rules and equitable principles as they apply in relation to directors and have effect in place of those rules and principles as regards the duties owed to a company by a director.

Section 170(4) of the CA 2006 states that

> The general duties shall be interpreted and applied in the same way as common law rules or equitable principles, and regard shall be had to the corresponding common law rules and equitable principles in interpreting and applying the general duties.

Thus, the existing case law continues to be vital in interpreting the law.

Under s 174 of the CA 2006 a director of a company must act with reasonable skill and care. The standard which is expected is that which would be exercised by a reasonably diligent person with:

(a) The general knowledge, skill and experience that may reasonably be expected of a person carrying out the functions carried out by the director; and

(b) The general knowledge, skill and experience that the director has.

The leading case is *Re City Equitable Fire and Insurance Co Ltd* [1925]. In this case, the company had experienced serious shortfalls of funds. The managing director, Mr Bevan was convicted of fraud. The liquidator sought to make other directors liable in negligence for failing to detect the frauds. Romer J, in what has become the classic exposition on the duty of care and skill, set out three propositions.

■ The first of these was

> A director need not exhibit in the performance of his duties a greater degree of skill than may be reasonably expected from a person of his knowledge and experience.

A director of a life insurance company, for instance, does not guarantee that he has the skill of an actuary or a physician. In the words of Lord Lindley MR, 'If the directors act within their powers, if they act with such care as is reasonably to be expected from them, having regard to their knowledge and experience, and if they act honestly for the benefit of the company they represent, they discharge both their equitable as well as their legal duty to the company' (*Lagunas Nitrate Co v Lagunas Syndicate* [1899]).

It is perhaps only another way of stating the same proposition to say that the directors are not liable for mere errors of judgment.

In relation to this principle, the decision in *Re Denham & Co* [1883] is illustrative. In this case, a director had recommended the payment of a dividend out of capital. The director was held not liable in negligence. It was stated that he was a country gentleman, not an accountant.

Section 13 of the Supply of Goods and Services Act 1982 introduced an implied term that the supplier of services would provide services of a reasonable standard. Directors were exempted from this provision before it came into force.

In *Dorchester Finance Co Ltd v Stebbing* [1989], Foster J held three directors liable for negligence. Two of the directors were non-executive directors and one was an executive director. The judge found that the duty that applied to the executive and non-executive directors was the same.

There are strong indications that the nature of the duty of care and skill is changing. Section 214 of the IA 1986, which is concerned with imposing liability for wrongful trading, provides for an objective standard of care in relation to directors and shadow directors where the company is insolvent and they ought to have recognised that fact. In some cases, it seems that s 214 of the IA 1986 has been used to try to establish an objective standard of care for

71

directors across the board. Thus, in *Norman v Theodore Goddard* [1991], Hoffmann J accepted that the standard in s 214 of the IA 1986 applied generally in relation to directors. The same judge in *Re D'Jan of London Ltd* [1994] accepted that the duty of care applicable was that set out in s 214 of the IA 1986. This objective standard is introduced in s 174 of the CA 2006.

In *Re Barings plc (No 5)* [2000], the judge, with whom the Court of Appeal agreed, stated that in the context of an application by the Secretary of State for a disqualification order under s 6 of the Company Directors Disqualification Act (CDDA) 1986, directors had, both collectively and individually, a continuing duty to acquire and maintain a sufficient knowledge and understanding of the company's business to enable them properly to discharge their duties as directors.

▓ The second proposition put forward by Romer J in *Re City Equitable* relates to the attention that has to be paid to the affairs of the company. He said:

> A director is not bound to give continuous attention to the affairs of a company. His duties are of an intermittent nature to be performed at periodic board meetings and at meetings of any committee of the board upon which he happens to be placed. He is not, however, bound to attend all such meetings, though he ought to attend whenever in the circumstances, he is reasonably able to do so.

An old illustration of this second proposition of Romer J is to be found in *Re Cardiff Savings Bank, Marquis of Bute's Case* [1892]. The Marquis of Bute was appointed president and director of the Cardiff Savings Bank when he was only six months old. During the next 38 years he attended only one board meeting. During this time frauds were perpetrated by another director. The court held that the Marquis was not liable for breach of duty in failing to attend board meetings as he had never undertaken to do so.

▓ The third proposition set out by Romer J is as follows:

> In respect of all duties that, having regard for the exigencies of business, and the articles of association, may properly be left to some other official, a director is, in the absence of grounds for suspicion, justified in trusting that official to perform such duties honestly . . .

This third proposition does not seem out of place today in the way that the other two propositions, which were first set out at the start of the 20th century, do.

In *Dovey v Cory* [1901], where a director had delegated the task of drawing up the accounts to others, it was held that he was entitled to rely on those accounts in recommending the payment of a dividend which was in fact made out of capital.

However, in *Re Barings plc (No 5)* [2000] the judge, with whom the Court of Appeal agreed, gave detailed consideration to the question of delegation and stated that, whilst directors were entitled to delegate particular functions to those below them in the management chain, and to trust their competence and integrity to a reasonable extent, the exercise of the power of delegation did not absolve a director from the duty to supervise the discharge of the delegated functions. The extent of any duty of supervision, and whether it has been discharged, depends on the facts of each particular case, including the director's role in the management of the company.

For another example, see *Cohen v Selby* [2001].

FIDUCIARY DUTIES

Other types of duties owed by directors are often described within the umbrella term 'fiduciary duties'. Much of this law has been developed by the cases, but these duties have now also been included within the Companies Act 2006.

Historically higher standards were expected of company directors in terms of honesty and integrity, since a director is considered to be a type of trustee of the company's property (*Keech v Sandford* [1726]; *JJ Harrison (Properties Ltd) v Harrison* [2001]).

The duty to promote the success of the company

At common law directors have been expected to act in a way that is *bona fide* for the benefit of the company. Section 172 of the CA 2006 put a director under a duty to promote the success of the company. However, the director's behaviour can be ratified by the company under s 239 of the CA 2006.

The duty to exercise independent judgment

At common law this is known as fettering a director's discretion. Section 173 CA 2006 is a statutory restatement of the common law (*Fulham Football Club and Others v Cabra Estates Plc* [1994]).

The duty to avoid conflicts of interest

This is set out in s 175 of the CA 2006.

1   A director of a company must avoid a situation in which he has, or can have, a direct or indirect interest that conflicts, or possibly may conflict, with the interests of the company.

2   This applies in particular to the exploitation of any property, information or opportunity (and it is immaterial whether the company could take advantage of the property, information or opportunity).

3   This duty does not apply to a conflict of interest arising in relation to a transaction or arrangement with the company.

4   This duty is not infringed—

   (a) if the situation cannot reasonably be regarded as likely to give rise to a conflict of interest; or

   (b) if the matter has been authorised by the directors.

It worth noting that other areas which are subject to director's fiduciary duties include:

(a) the power to borrow money and grant securities (*Rolled Steel Products (Holdings) Ltd v British Steel Corporation* [1986]);

(b) the power to make calls on partly paid shares;

(c) the power to call general meetings;

(d) the power to provide information to shareholders.

Transactions to which the company is a party

A director is under an obligation not to allow a conflict of interest to arise between his duty to the company and his own personal interest. This is now also covered by s 176 of the CA 2006. An example is where a director has an interest in a contract to which the company is a party, such as where the director has received an inducement from the other party to the contract, or where the director himself has entered into a contract with the company. Where a director places himself in such a position, he can be compelled by the company to account for any profit he made (*Boston Deep Sea Fishing Co v Ansell* [1888]). Further, a contract involving the company in which the director has an interest becomes voidable at the instance of the company (*Aberdeen Railway Co v*

Blaikie Bros [1854]; *Transvaal Lands Co v New Belgium (Transvaal) Land and Development Co* [1914]). An alternative remedy to an account for profit is for the company to seek damages against the director for any loss the company has suffered as a result of the conflict of interest (*Mahesan v Malaysia Government Officers' Co-operative Housing Society Ltd* [1979]; *Coleman Taymar Ltd v Oakes* [2001]). In *Attorney-General for Hong Kong v Reid* [1994], the Privy Council recognised a proprietary remedy by way of a constructive trust in favour of the company against the director or other agent in respect of the bribe, so that the company would be able to claim any profit the director made from the use of the bribe.

In addition to the general equitable rules, certain provisions of the CA 2006 require a director to make disclosures. Section 182(1) of the CA 2006 requires the director to disclose any interest that he has in a contract between himself and the company. The provision extends to connected persons. Connected persons are the director's spouse or infant children, a company with whom the director is associated (that is to say, he controls more than 20 per cent of the voting capital), a trustee of a trust whose beneficiaries include the director himself or a connected person, a partner of the director or of a connected person (s 252 of the CA 2006).

A shadow director is also required to comply with s 182 of the CA 2006 in the same way as a director. Disclosure under s 182 of the CA 2006 should be to the full board. The section is not complied with by disclosing the matter to a sub-committee of the board (*Guinness plc v Saunders* [1990]).

Mere compliance with the section does not entitle a director to keep any profits. In order to keep the profit, the director must either rely on a provision in the company's constitution or have his retention of the profit ratified by the company in general meeting (*North-West Transportation Co Ltd v Beatty* [1887]).

Fair dealing provisions

Some contracts require prior authorisation by the company in general meeting regardless of what the company's articles provide. Section 190(1) of the CA 2006 applies to what are termed substantial property transactions. If the director or shadow director is to sell to or purchase from the company one or more non-cash assets that are substantial, prior approval in general meeting is needed. A transaction is substantial if the market value of the asset exceeds the lower of £100,000 or 10 per cent of the company's net asset value (as set out in the last balance sheet). Transactions worth less than £2,000 are not substantial. Section 190(1) of the CA 2006 applies, just as s 182(1) of the CA 2006 does, to connected persons.

If the substantial property transaction does not receive prior authorisation or ratification within a reasonable period of its conclusion, it is voidable at the instance of the company. The director concerned is liable to make good any profit to the company and to indemnify the company against any loss (see *Re Duckwari plc* [1999]). Note also s 188(1) of the CA 2006, which requires approval of the general meeting for a director's contract of employment lasting more than two years (see *Runciman v Walter Runciman plc* [1992]).

Section 41 of the CA 2006 provides that where the third party to a transaction with a company is a director of that company, or its holding company, or is connected to the director, and the transaction is beyond the powers of the board of directors under the company's constitution, the contract becomes voidable at the instance of the company. The section further provides that the third party or those directors who authorised the transaction are liable to indemnify the company for any loss or damage resulting from the transaction and to account to the company for any gain made from the transaction.

Section 231(1) of the CA 2006 provides that the terms of a contract between a single member company and its sole member, who is also a director of the company, shall, unless the contract is in writing, either be set out in a written memorandum or be recorded in the minutes of the first meeting of the directors of the company following the making of the contract.

Under s 378 of the CA 2006 donations by a company to political parties that exceed £5,000 or any expenditure on its own political activities must be authorised by a resolution of members. If a contribution or expenditure is made without authority, the directors at the time are liable to reimburse the company, with interest.

Transactions to which the company is not a party

In respect of corporate property, such as corporate opportunities, a director must not place himself in a position where his duty to the company conflicts with his personal interest. If he does, he is obliged to favour the interest of the company rather than his own. The leading case in this area is *Regal (Hastings) Ltd v Gulliver* [1942]. Regal owned a cinema in Hastings. The company's solicitor, Garston, thought that it would be a sound business proposition to acquire two other cinemas in the town. He suggested this to the board of directors. The company itself could not afford the purchase. However, a scheme was devised where the company's solicitor, the directors and the company itself would each put up some of the funds for the purchase. The move was a successful one and the company prospered. Ultimately, the company was sold as a going concern to a purchaser. He purchased the company's shares. The company under its new management then commenced an action against the erstwhile directors for damages in respect of the profit that they had made on the sale of their shares. It was established that the directors had acted from prudent financial motives and there was no *mala fides.* The House of Lords held, however, that the directors had acquired the shares in exploitation of their position as directors. The key issue is whether the director has made the profit in question 'by reason and by virtue' of his position as director. They had not obtained the consent of the company and were bound to disgorge the profit back to the company. It was unfortunate that the company had been sold as a going concern and thus the purchaser was in the position to bring the action. If the company's assets had been sold, as opposed to the shares in the company, the purchaser would have had no *locus standi* to bring the action.

The same principle is borne out in later decisions. In *Industrial Development Consultants v Cooley* [1972], Cooley had been an architect with the East Midlands Gas Board. He left there to become a director of IDC. Whilst there, he was approached by the Gas Board. They wished him to design a gas holder for them at Ponders End. They did not wish to deal with IDC. They made it quite clear that the offer was only an offer to Cooley personally. Cooley went to his management and told them, dishonestly, that he was desperately ill and sought leave to terminate his contract. This was agreed to. He then contracted with the Gas Board, making a profit from the design of the gas holder. The judge said that the profit that he had made on the contract should be disgorged back to IDC. He held that it was a corporate opportunity which had come his way by virtue of his office of director, even though it was one which the company was unlikely to obtain. Similarly, in *Canadian Aero Service Ltd v O'Malley* [1972], the director was held liable for depriving the company of a 'maturing business activity'. See also *Gencor ACP Ltd v Dalby* [2000]; *CMS Dolphin Ltd v Simonet* [2001]; *Bhullar v Bhullar* [2003]; *Item Software (UK) v Fassihi* [2004].

A further decision in the same area is *Horcal Ltd v Gatland* [1984]. Gatland, a director of the company, was close to retirement. The board of directors had decided to award him a golden handshake. After the decision had been reached, Gatland took a phone call from a potential customer of the company. He converted the business to his own account. This came to light later when the customer rang the company to complain about the quality of the work. The company brought this action, partly to obtain disgorgement of the profit made and partly to obtain a return of the golden handshake payment. The company succeeded in obtaining disgorgement of the profit. It would have been surprising had they not so succeeded. They did not obtain a return of the golden handshake payment, however. It was held that this payment had been decided prior to the director diverting the contract.

In *Cranleigh Precision Engineering Ltd v Bryant* [1965], the director concerned had been working on a revolutionary above-ground swimming pool. He left the company, taking plans with him and developed a swimming pool of his own based on the plans. The company brought the action to seek disgorgement of profits that he had made and was successful.

However, the company was not successful with its action in *Balston Ltd v Headline Filters Ltd* [1990]. H was a former employee and director of the plaintiff company, for whom he had worked for 17 years. Before giving notice to the company, terminating his employment and directorship, he had entered into a private lease agreement in respect of premises where he intended to set up his own business. After leaving the company, one of the company's customers telephoned H, after being informed by the company that the company would only be able to supply the customer with a particular kind of filter tube for a limited period of time. As a result of this call, H commenced business making the filter tubes for the customer. The court held that there was no breach of fiduciary duty. The general fiduciary duties of a director or employee did not prevent that person, while still a director or employee, from forming the intention to set up in competition once his employment had ceased, or indeed from taking preliminary steps to forward that intention, provided there was no actual competitive activity, such as competitive tendering or actual trading, while the directorship or employment continued.

In *Coleman Taymar Ltd v Oakes* [2001], the court held that the director's actions, in indirectly purchasing unwanted equipment belonging to the company while still employed by the company, went beyond the taking of preliminary steps towards the commencement of a competing business. In *LC Services Ltd v Brown* [2003], it was held that a director, who had during the course of employment delivered a copy of the company's electronic database to a rival company for which he worked, had acted in breach of duty. He had also removed company documents and had copied some of the company's maintenance procedures which constituted confidential information.

Not every case of a director taking an opportunity that has come by way of the company will involve a breach of duty. If the company has turned down the opportunity without any improper influence from the director and the director takes it up subsequently, there is no reason why the director should not retain the profit. In *Peso Silver Mines v Cropper* [1966], before the Supreme Court of Canada, the court held that a director was entitled to keep a profit in these circumstances. Other examples can be found in *Queensland Mines Ltd v Hudson* [1978] and *Island Export Finance Ltd v Umunna* [1986]. In *Queensland Mines*, the managing director of a company was held not liable to account for the profit he made on an opportunity that came his way as managing director of the company, as the company's board of directors had renounced the company's interest in the venture and had assented to the managing director's activities.

In *Island Export Finance Ltd v Umunna* [1986], the judge said the question of whether a director was liable to disgorge a profit to his former company from a corporate opportunity was to some extent a question of timing. The director in this case had resigned from the company in order to set up in business on his own account. In addition, at the time, there were no specific corporate opportunities. It was held that in these circumstances Umunna could take the business that came his way.

The area of corporate opportunities is a fertile one for examiners, particularly in relation to problem questions. This area, therefore, deserves special attention.

A related area is the question of competition: to what extent is a director of the company able to compete with the company of which he is a director, either through another company or a partnership, or as a sole trader? The old British case of *London and Mashonaland Exploration Co Ltd v New Mashonaland Exploration Co Ltd* [1891] puts forward the proposition that it does not involve a breach of duty. The decision is surprising although it was approved *obiter* by

Lord Blanesburgh in *Bell v Lever Bros* [1932]. Note also *Plus Group Ltd v Pyke* [2002].

However, if a corporate opportunity comes the way of a director, and he is a director of two companies, he will inevitably be in breach of fiduciary duty, should he divert the opportunity from one company to the other (see the conflicting views of the members of the Court of Appeal in *Coleman Taymar Ltd v Oakes* [2001]).

Commonwealth authority is inconsistent on the point. Some cases follow the *Mashonaland* decision. Others indicate that directors cannot compete with the companies they serve (see *Abbey Glen Property Corp v Stumborg* [1975]).

In some areas of British law, there is an indication that competition is not permissible. In *Hivac Ltd v Park Royal Scientific Instruments Ltd* [1946], senior employees engaged on sensitive work in wartime were not able to compete with their employer. Admittedly this is a special decision and, this decision apart, it is perhaps more appropriate for the courts to draw a parallel with the law relating to employees and restraint of trade claims.

The duty to act within powers

Under s 171 of the CA 2006 this duty has two parts. The director must act in accordance with the company's constitution and then only exercise powers for the purpose for which they were conferred. A good example, in relation to companies with a share capital, is the power to issue shares.

This power is given for the purpose of raising necessary capital for the running of the company (*Punt v Symons* [1903]). If this is the purpose for which it is used, it is clearly a valid exercise of the power. Other purposes, such as, for example, staving off an unwelcome takeover bid, even if the directors are *bona fide* of the view that it is in the company's best interests not to be taken over, will be a wrongful use of the power. However, the shareholders (excluding those holding the disputed shares) can ratify the issue in general meeting. This was the case in *Hogg v Cramphorn Ltd* [1967] and *Bamford v Bamford* [1970].

If the exercise of the power is for some extraneous purpose to benefit the directors and not to benefit the company, then the issue of the shares cannot be validated by the company in general meeting (see *Howard Smith Ltd v Ampol Petroleum Ltd* [1974]).

If an issue of shares is made to disturb an existing balance of control within a company, then it may be held invalid. This happened in *Pennell Securities Ltd v Venida Investments Ltd* [1974]. Similarly, in *Clemens v Clemens Bros Ltd* [1976], an issue of shares made to dilute the voting power of one shareholder was held invalid.

Thus, directors' powers must be exercised in a fiduciary way. This is illustrated by those cases concerning the issue of shares but may be demonstrated in other areas. In *Re Smith and Fawcett Ltd* [1942], the same principle applied in relation to the directors' power to refuse to register a transfer of shares. It also applied in relation to entry into a management agreement in *Lee Panavision Ltd v Lee Lighting Ltd* [1992].

Nor should it be forgotten that, where there is no breach of a director's duties, there may still be a shareholders' petition under s 994(1) of the CA 2006.

In connection with director's powers it is worth noting that the provisions of the Bribery Act 2010 came into operation from July 2011. This act outlawed the giving of financial or any other kind or advantage which would encourage a person to carry out their activities improperly or to reward a person for having done so. A company could be held liable for the acts of its directors if they commit this offence unless it can be shown that adequate procedures were in place to prevent bribery from taking place.

CORPORATE GOVERNANCE

Corporate governance is defined as 'the system by which companies are directed and controlled'. Corporate governance goes beyond the legal obligations of directors and includes the idea of accountability of directors to shareholders.

There were a series of reports during the 1990s (Cadbury, Greenbury, and Hampel), which focused on how plcs were being run. The result of these investigations was the Combined Code on corporate governance. The Code covers the responsibilities of the directors and the board as a whole and the responsibilities of the shareholders.

There have been further reviews of the area (Turnbull, Higgs, Smith and Tyson). These reports have examined the role and effectiveness of the non executive directors and investigated how the pool of talent can be expanded. The

Combined Code was revised to take into account the findings of the latest reports.

The current version of the Code is now The UK Corporate Governance Code which was revised and reissued in 2010. All companies with a Premium Listing of equity shares in the UK are required under the Listing Rules to report on how they have applied the Combined Code in their annual report and accounts. Currently there is consultation ongoing regarding gender diversity and improving women's representation on boards following the Davies Report in 2011.

Directors' duties – summary

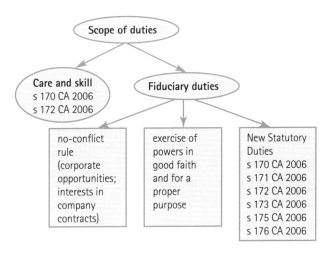

CONCLUSION

The area of directors' duties is a vital one. Unlike some areas of company law, which are self-contained and may lend themselves to strategic omission, you must learn this topic.

DISQUALIFICATION OF DIRECTORS

The court is given the power under the Company Directors Disqualification Act (CDDA) 1986 to make an order against a person that he or she shall not, without leave of the court, be a director of a company or in any way, whether directly or indirectly, be concerned or take part in the promotion, formation or management of a company. There are a number of grounds on which an order can be made, eg where a person is convicted of an indictable offence in connection with the promotion, formation, management or liquidation of a company (s 2 of the CDDA 1986), or where a person is in persistent breach of the companies legislation in respect of filing of accounts (s 3 of the CDDA 1986).

The most important ground is contained in s 6 of the CDDA 1986 which provides that a court must make a disqualification order against a person where it is satisfied that that person has been a director of a company which has become insolvent and that his conduct as a director makes him unfit to be concerned in the management of a company. The minimum order under this section is two years and the maximum is 15 years.

In *Re Sevenoaks Stationers (Retail) Ltd* [1991] Dillon LJ said that the purpose of s 6 of the CDDA 1986 is to protect the public by ensuring that creditors do not lose money through companies becoming insolvent where the directors of those companies are unfit to be concerned in the management of a company. His Lordship gave guidelines for the courts to use when determining the period of disqualification:

> . . . (i) the top bracket of disqualification for periods of over 10 years should be reserved for particularly severe cases. These may include cases where a director who has already had one period of disqualification imposed on him falls to be disqualified yet again. (ii) The minimum bracket of two to five years' disqualification should be applied where, though disqualification is mandatory, the case is, relatively, not very serious. (iii) The middle bracket of disqualification from six to 10 years should apply for serious cases which do not merit the top bracket.

In *Secretary of State for Trade and Industry v McTighe (No. 2)* [1996], the Court of Appeal imposed a disqualification of 12 years on a director who had caused three successive companies to trade at the risk of creditors, leaving unpaid debts of £1m. The director had misappropriated £0.5m from the company and had failed persistently to co-operate with the liquidator and the official receiver.

In relation to a charge of unfitness against a director, the court is required by s 9 of the CDDA 1986 to have regard to the matters specified in Part I of Sched 1 to the CDDA 1986 which include any misfeasance or breach of duty in relation to the company; any misapplication of company property; and the extent of any responsibility for any failure by the company to comply with accounting and publicity requirements of the CA 2006. Where the company has become insolvent, the court is to have regard to the matters listed in Part II of Sched 1 to the CDDA 1986 and these include the extent of a director's responsibility for the causes of the company becoming insolvent and the extent of a director's responsibility for any failure by the company to supply any goods or services which have been paid for.

Whether or not a director's conduct makes him unfit is a question of fact, but such conduct has been described as involving 'a lack of commercial probity' (*Re Lo-Line Electric Motors Ltd* [1988]), 'a serious failure or serious failures' of duty 'whether deliberately or through incompetence' (*Re Bath Glass Ltd* [1988]), or falling 'below the standards of probity and competence appropriate for persons fit to be directors of companies' (*Re Grayan Building Services Ltd* [1995]).

Acting in contravention of a disqualification order is an offence triable either way (s 13 of the CDDA 2006) and such a person can be made liable for the debts and liabilities of the company that arose while acting in contravention of a disqualification order (s 15 of the CDDA 1986).

Under the CDDA 1986, as amended by the IA 2000, the Secretary of State can accept an undertaking from a director that he consents to a period of disqualification, if considered expedient in the public interest (ss 7(2A), 8(2A) of the CDDA 1986). This measure is designed to reduce the cost and length of disqualification proceedings. The penalties for breaking a disqualification undertaking are the same as for acting contrary to a disqualification order.

Under s 9A of the CDDA 1986, a disqualification order must be made against a person who has been a director of a company which has breached competition law where the director's conduct makes him unfit to be concerned with the management of a company.

A register of disqualification orders and undertakings is maintained at Companies House and can be inspected free of charge.

THE COMPANY SECRETARY

HISTORY

- *Barnett Hoares & Co v South London Tramways Co* [1887].

- *Panorama Developments (Guildford Ltd) v Fidelis Furnishing Fabrics Ltd* [1971].

Under ss 270 and 271 of the CA 2006 private companies are no longer required to have a company secretary.

DUTIES OF THE COMPANY SECRETARY

- The company secretary owes fiduciary duties (see *Re Morvah Consols Tin Mining Co* [1875]).

RESPONSIBILITIES OF THE COMPANY SECRETARY

- Preparation and keeping of minutes (s 248 of the CA 2006).

- Dealing with share transfers and issuing share and debenture certificates.

- Keeping and maintaining the register of members and debenture holders (s 113(1) and s 743(6) of the CA 2006).

- Keeping and maintaining the register of directors and secretary (s 162(1) of the CA 2006).

- The registration of charges and the maintaining of the company's register of charges (s 860(1) and s 876(1) of the CA 2006).

- Keeping and maintaining the register of directors' share interests (s 809 of the CA 2006).

- Keeping of records of directors' service contracts (s 228(1) of the CA 2006).

- The collation of directors' interests that have to be disclosed (s 412(5) of the CA 2006).

- Keeping and maintaining the register of material share interests (s 808(1) of the CA 2006).

- Sending notices of meetings, copies of accounts, etc.

- Keeping the company's constitution up to date.

- Preparation and submission of the annual return (ss 854–857 of the CA 2006).

- Filing of necessary documents.

- Witnessing documents together with a director.

- Payment of dividends and the preparation of dividend warrants.

It may be that other duties fall upon the company secretary as well, matters such as employment issues, dealing with the accountants, obtaining legal advice from the solicitors and dealing with the Financial Services Authority if this is appropriate.

QUALIFICATIONS OF THE COMPANY SECRETARY

Section 273 of the CA 2006 lays down requirements for company secretaries of public companies. No statutory qualifications need to be held by the company secretary of a private company.

POWERS OF THE COMPANY SECRETARY

> ... times have changed. A company secretary is a much more important person nowadays than he was in 1887 (*Panorama Developments (Guildford) Ltd v Fidelis Furnishing Fabrics Ltd* [1971], *per* Lord Denning MR).

In this case, the increased status of the company secretary was relevant to finding that here the secretary had ostensible authority to enter into contracts of an administrative nature on behalf of the company.

AUDITORS

The objects of an audit were set out by Lord Denning in *Fomento (Sterling Area) Ltd v Selsdon Fountain Pen Co Ltd* [1988], as follows:

- to verify arithmetical accuracy;

- to make checks to establish that the accounts do not mask errors or dishonesty;

- reporting on the accounts as to whether they provide reliable information respecting the true financial position of the company.

NATURE OF POST OF AUDITOR

The provisions relating to the qualification, appointment, removal, resignation and remuneration of auditors are found in ss 485–520 of the CA 2006. The nature of the auditors' reports, including the duties of auditors, is set out in sections 475, 459, 498 of the CA 2006. Additional provisions relating to the independence of auditors and auditor regulation, when in force, are contained in the Companies (Audit, Investigations and Community Enterprise) Act 2004.

LIABILITY OF AUDITORS

Section 532 of the CA 2006 restricts the ability of a company in its articles of association from exempting an auditor from liability for negligence. But s 1157 of the CA 2006 does allow the court to relieve an auditor from liability if he has acted honestly and fairly and if he ought reasonably to be excused.

Tortious liability

- *Hedley Byrne v Heller* [1964].

- *JEB Fasteners Ltd v Marks Bloom & Co (A Firm)* [1983].

- *Caparo Industries plc v Dickman and Others* [1990].

- *Morgan Crucible Co plc v Hill Samuel & Co Ltd* [1991].

- *Berg Sons & Co Ltd v Adams* [1993].

- *Galoo Ltd v Bright Grahame Murray* [1994].

- *BCCI (Overseas) Ltd v Price Waterhouse* [1999].

- *Barings plc (in liq) v Coopers Lybrand (a firm)* [2002].

Auditors' statutory liability

- Section 212 of the IA 1986, for misapplication of company property or misfeasance in connection with breach of any fiduciary or other duty owed to the company.

You should now be confident that you would be able to tick all of the boxes on the checklist at the beginning of this chapter. To check your knowledge of The management of the company why not visit the companion website and take the Multiple Choice Question test. Check your understanding of the terms and vocabulary used in this chapter with the flashcard glossary.

Company meetings

5

MEETINGS

ANNUAL GENERAL MEETINGS

Section 336 of the Companies Act (CA) 2006 requires public companies to hold an annual general meeting in every calendar year. Private companies do not have to hold an AGM. It may use written resolutions instead.

EXTRAORDINARY GENERAL MEETINGS

These may be called as follows:

Section 303 of the CA 2006 allows two or more members holding 10 per cent of the shareholding to requisition the calling of an extraordinary general meeting.

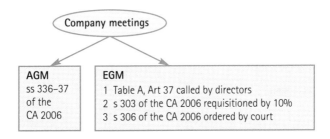

THE CONDUCT OF MEETINGS

Notice

Length of notice

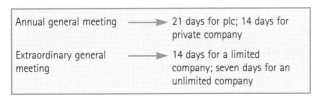

If a special resolution is to be proposed, 21 days' notice is required.

Section 307 of the CA 2006 allows meetings to be called at short notice in certain circumstances.

Contents

The notice must clearly set out the date, time and place of the meeting. It should also set out the text of any resolution to be proposed.

If the meeting is an annual general meeting, the notice must say so.

The right to appoint a proxy and that that proxy need not be a member should always be set out. More than one proxy can be appointed (ss 324–331 of the CA 2006).

Serving the notice

Section 310(1) of the CA 2006 provides that the notice should be served in the manner required by Table A. This applies if there is no contrary provision.

The chairman

Section 319 of the CA 2006 sets out the procedure for electing a chairman of the meeting. This no longer has to be the chairman of the board. It could be a member or a proxy.

The chairman is responsible for taking the meeting through the agenda, for putting matters to the vote and for keeping order (*John v Rees* [1969]).

The chairman's declaration of the result of any vote is conclusive in the absence of fraud or obvious mistake (*Re Caratal (New) Mines Ltd* [1902]).

Quorum

Section 318(2) of the CA 2006 provides for a quorum of two members unless the company's articles provide otherwise.

On the problem of meetings of one person, see *Sharp v Dawes* [1876]; *Re Sanitary Carbon Co* [1877]; *Re London Flats Ltd* [1969].

Sometimes, meetings may have to be held with one member, as follows:

- Class meeting of one (*East v Bennett Brothers* [1911]).

- Private companies with only one member (s 318(1) of the CA 2006).

- A meeting ordered by the court under s 306 of the CA 2006 where the quorum is fixed at one (see *Re Sticky Fingers Restaurant Ltd* [1992]).

It would appear that meetings can be held validly even though the members are not all in each other's physical presence if there is an effective audio/visual link (see *Byng v London Life Association Ltd* [1990]).

Calling meetings – summary

- Appropriate length of notice
- Correct details in notice
- Chairman of the meeting must be properly appointed
- Must be an appropriate quorum for the meeting

Special notice

Special notice is defined in s 312 of the CA 2006. It is 28 days' notice of a resolution given to the company by a member. It is needed in two situations:

the removal of a director under s 168 of the CA 2006;

the removal of an auditor under s 511 of the CA 2006.

Resolutions

The law relating to resolutions has been changed by CA 2006. Private companies can pass resolutions either via written resolution (s 281(1)(a) of the CA 2006) or at a member's meeting (s 281(1)(b) of the CA 2006). Under s 282 of the CA 2006 written resolutions can now be passed by a simple majority.

Special resolution

This is one passed by a majority of at least 75 per cent of those voting after 21 days' notice (s 283 of the CA 2006), eg a resolution to change the company's articles of association.

Ordinary resolution

This is defined in s 282 of the CA 2006 as a resolution passed by a simple majority of those voting. It will usually involve 14 days' notice.

On occasion, the courts have been willing to apply 'the assent principle' to unanimity where there has been no meeting regardless of the type of company involved (see *Re Express Engineering Works Ltd* [1920]).

Elective resolution

These have been abolished by CA 2006.

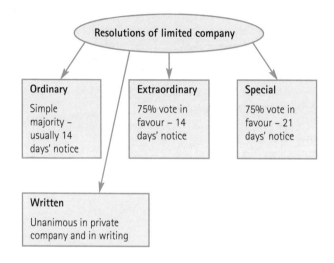

Unanimous informal consent

Where there has been no formal resolution passed at a general meeting, if it can be shown that all the shareholders with the right to attend and vote at a general meeting have assented to some matter at a meeting or which is not within the powers of the general meeting to carry into effect, such assent is as binding as a resolution passed in a properly convened general meeting (*Re Duomatic Ltd* [1969]). This principle has been applied in cases where there was a technical requirement for the general meeting to waive failures to comply with formalities (*Re Express Engineering Works Ltd* [1920]; *Re Oxted Motor Co Ltd* [1921]) and cases involving an approval of directors' remuneration (*Re Duomatic Ltd* [1969] and a director's service contract under s 188 of the CA 2006 (*Atlas Wright (Europe) Ltd v Wright* [1999]). The principle has also enabled a shareholders' agreement to vary the provisions of a company's articles which would normally require the passing of a special resolution (*Cane v Jones* [1980]). However, the principle can be applied only to transactions which are *intra vires* the company (*Ultraframe (UK) Ltd v Fielding* [2003]).

Votes

The Companies Act 2006 sets out a minimum standard for the conduct votes in s 321. Votes are conducted first on a show of hands with one vote per member, proxies not voting unless the articles so provide. A poll may be demanded by any five members (here proxies count) or 10 per cent of the voting rights. A decision on a poll will override a decision on a show of hands.

Adjournment

At common law, there is a power to adjourn if there is disorder or if there is a problem accommodating all those turning up.

Minutes

Companies must keep minutes of all general meetings (s 248 of the CA 2006).

You should now be confident that you would be able to tick all of the boxes on the checklist at the beginning of this chapter. To check your knowledge of Company meetings why not visit the companion website and take the Multiple Choice Question test. Check your understanding of the terms and vocabulary used in this chapter with the flashcard glossary.

6

Shareholder protection

INTRODUCTION

The protection of shareholder interests and, in particular, minority shareholder interests, is of fundamental importance. The position of the majority shareholders is usually better in that, as mentioned elsewhere, they have the power to dismiss the directors under s 168 of the Companies Act (CA) 2006.

MAJORITY CONTROL – MINORITY PROTECTION

INTRODUCTION

There are several areas that need to be looked at in the context of minority protection. The first of these is the statutory derivative claim, which effectively replaces the rule in *Foss v Harbottle* [1843] and the exceptions to that rule. The statutory remedy for members who are unfairly prejudiced in the conduct of the company's affairs remains (ss 994–996 of the CA 2006) as does the possibility that a shareholder may petition the court for a winding up order, under s 122 of the Insolvency Act (IA) 1986.

THE STATUTORY DERIVATIVE CLAIM

The Companies Act 2006 introduced a new basis for the derivative claim under s 260. Now any derivative claim is brought under Part 11 by a member of the company in respect of a cause of action vested in the company and the relief must be sought on behalf of the company. A derivative claim may be brought against the directors or another person but only 'in respect of a cause of action arising from an actual or proposed act or omission involving negligence, default, breach of duty or breach of trust by a director of a company' (s 260(3)).

There are safeguards written into the CA 2006 to prevent vexatious or frivolous claims. Under s 261 there is a two stage process to bringing a claim. First, the applicant must show that they have a *prima facie* case. The court will consider the application and evidence filed by the applicants. If the court does not find that a prima facie cases exists, then the application must be dismissed. If a prima facie case does exist then there is a full hearing to see whether permission to continue the claim should be given. The court is required to consider various factors in deciding whether to let the claim proceed, including whether any breach is likely to be ratified (s 263(3)).

If the claim is successful, any compensation will go to the company but the claimant will recover costs.

The case law to date on derivative claims is mixed. In *Iesini v Westrip Holdings Ltd* [2010] the two stage procedure was followed. But in other cases where the court has sought to avoid unnecessary delay and cost the hearing has been treated as the second stage of the application with the defendants' consent (*Franbar Holdings Ltd v Patel* [2009], *Mission Capital Plc v Sinclair* [2010]). In *Stimpson v Southern Landlords Association* [2010] the court proceeded direct to the hearing despite objections from the defendants. *Iesini* conflicts with the approach taken in the Scottish case of *Wishart v Castlecroft Securities Ltd* [2010] when determining the threshold for a *prima facie* case. In *Wishart* this appeared to be placing the onus on the court to effuse the application if there is not a *prima facie* case but in *Iesini* it was stated that a *prima facie* case 'necessarily entails a decision that there is a *prima facie* case both that the company has a good cause of action and that the cause of action arises out of a directors' default'.

It appears that the hurdle of establishing a *prima facie* case is proving difficult for many claimants to clear. To date only two cases (*Kiani v Cooper* [2010] and *Stainer v Lee* [2010]) have gone to trial but only after disclosure.

The Derivative Case Law
The case law is still instructive even though the common law action has now been superceded as it provides some guidance in respect of overseas companies and multiple derivative claims where a statutory derivative claim can not be brought.

The decision in *Foss v Harbottle* concerned park land in Moss Side, Manchester, which was a leafy suburb of the city. Businessmen in the city had grouped together to purchase land to dedicate to the then heiress to the throne, Princess Victoria. The park opened to great rejoicing. Difficulties soon followed. Some of the company's members alleged that certain directors had misapplied company property. It was alleged that the directors had taken, for themselves, out of the monies of the company, a price exceeding the value of the land. The Vice-Chancellor, Wigram VC, held that the action could not proceed. The wrong, if a wrong existed at all, had been done not to individual shareholders but to the company. Wigram said:

The Victoria Park Company is an incorporated body, and the conduct with which the defendants are charged in this suit is an injury not to the plaintiffs exclusively; it is an injury to the whole corporation by individuals whom the corporation entrusted with powers to be exercised only for the good of the corporation.

▶ FOSS v HARBOTTLE [1843]

Businessmen in the city had grouped together to purchase land to dedicate to Princess Victoria. Some of the company's members alleged that certain directors had misapplied company property. It was alleged that the directors had taken, for themselves, out of the monies of the company, a price exceeding the value of the land. The Vice-Chancellor, Wigram VC, held that the action could not proceed. The wrong, if a wrong existed at all, had been done not to individual shareholders but to the company.

Wigram said:

The Victoria Park Company is an incorporated body, and the conduct with which the defendants are charged in this suit is an injury not to the plaintiffs exclusively; it is an injury to the whole corporation by individuals whom the corporation entrusted with powers to be exercised only for the good of the corporation.

The case gives some indication of the types of situation where the new statutory law could be used.

This principle – the rule in *Foss v Harbottle* – has acted like a dead hand on minority protection in British company law. The rule may be justified. A company in general meeting may ratify what has been done and that might, therefore, make litigation pointless. Another possible ground on which the decision may be justified is that it prevents a multiplicity of actions, because a number of shareholders may wish to complain about what has been done in the name of the company.

The principle in *Foss v Harbottle* was applied in *MacDougall v Gardiner* [1875]. In this case, some shareholders complained that the company, the Silver Mining

Company Ltd, had failed to hold special general meetings. The Court of Appeal held that no proceedings could be brought to complain about a matter which amounted to a procedural irregularity since this was a matter which was within the competence of the majority to ratify and approve.

There are certain established exceptions to the principle in *Foss v Harbottle*. The areas of exception were set out with clarity in the judgment of Jenkins LJ in *Edwards v Halliwell* [1950] as follows.

An *ultra vires* act

If the complaint by a shareholder is that the company has engaged in an *ultra vires* activity, a minority action, as an exception to *Foss v Harbottle*, has been permitted. It used to be the case that *ultra vires* activities could not be ratified. Thus, in *Parke v Daily News Ltd* [1962], a single shareholder was able to bring an action to restrain the company from giving gratuitous payments to employees in excess of those to which they were entitled by law or under contract. Similarly, in *Simpson v Westminster Palace Hotel Co* [1868], a shareholder was able to bring an action complaining that the company was acting *ultra vires* in proposing to use hotel rooms for offices.

The special majorities exception

Where a company's constitution stipulates that a special majority is needed before a particular course of action can be accomplished, if the company seeks to flout this without obtaining the required majority, a single shareholder may maintain an action as an exception to *Foss v Harbottle*. This was the case in *Edwards v Halliwell* [1950], a case which in fact concerns a point of trade union law rather than company law, but in this area the principles are identical. The National Union of Vehicle Builders had a provision in its rule book that stated that the members' subscriptions could only be increased by a ballot vote of members resulting in a two thirds majority for the proposal. In contravention of this provision, a delegate meeting purported to increase the subscription. A branch of the union objected. The Court of Appeal held that the rule in *Foss v Harbottle* could not be relied upon in this instance. It was a recognised exception to the rule that where a particular majority was required and that majority had not been obtained, then an individual member may bring an action as an exception to *Foss v Harbottle*.

The personal rights exception

Where a company denies a member rights that are set out in the company's constitution, the member may maintain an action as an exception to *Foss v Harbottle*. Thus, in *Pender v Lushington* [1877], a shareholder was able to enforce his right and that of other shareholders that they should be able to cast their votes. In *Wood v Odessa Waterworks* [1889], a shareholder was able to enforce his right to a dividend to be paid in cash rather than in property where this was provided for under the company's articles. However, the courts have not been prepared to recognise a personal right where there has been a mere informality or irregularity which the majority of the members is capable of rectifying (*MacDougall v Gardiner* [1875]). The courts have also held that a member cannot bring a personal claim for the loss in value of his shares which has arisen from the damage caused to the company by a wrongdoer, as that loss is merely a reflection of the loss suffered by the company (*Prudential Assurance Co Ltd v Newman Industries Ltd (No 2)* [1982]; *Stein v Blake* [1997]; *Johnson v Gore Wood* [2001]; *Barings plc v Coopers Lybrand (a firm)* [2001]; *Gardner v Parker* [2003]). However, in *Giles v Rhind* [2002], the Court of Appeal held that where the company was unable to bring an action because of the conduct of the wrongdoer, the reflective loss rule did not apply and, therefore, so long as a shareholder had a separate cause of action, he could bring a personal claim in such circumstances.

Fraud on the minority

The most important exception to the rule in *Foss v Harbottle* is where fraud has been perpetrated by those in control of the company. It seemed from the first instance judgment in *Prudential Assurance v Newman Industries* [1980] that 'those in control' may mean those in day to day management control who might not have a controlling majority of votes in general meeting, but this was disapproved of by the Court of Appeal *obiter*. It is submitted that the better view is that 'control' means a majority of votes in general meeting.

Fraud may never be ratified. The objection to a single member bringing an action on behalf of all members where the conduct complained of may be subsequently ratified does not therefore apply in this instance. Thus, in *Cook v Deeks* [1916], a Privy Council case on appeal from Ontario, a shareholder was able to bring an action under this head complaining that directors had diverted corporate opportunities away from the company to themselves personally. The exception is limited to cases of fraud. It does not apply in cases of negligence where the controllers of the company have not themselves benefited, for example, *Pavlides v Jensen* [1956], where the complaint was that the directors had been negligent in selling an asbestos mine in Cyprus at an under-valuation. Similarly, in *Heyting v Dupont* [1964], the complaint was one of negligence, not one of fraud, and so the action could not proceed. But contrast this with the decision in *Daniels v Daniels* [1978]. In this case, the complaint was framed as one of negligence. It concerned a purchase by a director of property from the company for £4,250 and its subsequent re-sale for some £120,000 by the director concerned. Templeman J allowed the action to proceed. He said that mere negligence is one thing but negligence with such a massive profit to the negligent party is quite another thing. Thus, so-called 'self-serving' negligence can constitute 'fraud'.

Another interesting case is *Estmanco (Kilner House) Ltd v Greater London Council* [1982]. In this case, the shareholders in the company had no voting rights. They were leaseholders in a block of flats. Voting control was vested in the local authority. The management agreement provided that the council would use its best endeavours to sell the flats. Subsequently, there was a change of political control of the council. The council decided not to proceed with sale of the properties. One of the leaseholders, who was a member of the company, sought to proceed with this action. Megarry VC held that this case fell within 'the fraud on the minority' exception since the action taken by the local authority, as the majority shareholder, in preventing the company from bringing legal proceedings, frustrated the whole purpose underlying the company's existence.

These actions brought by shareholders under the fraud on the minority exception are known as 'derivative claims' since the shareholder is exceptionally being allowed to bring an action to pursue a right belonging to the company itself.

It is possible for a shareholder bringing a derivative claim to claim an indemnity for costs incurred in the litigation from the company (*Wallersteiner v Moir (No 2)* [1974]; *Civil Procedure Rules 1998*). The action has to be one which a reasonable independent board would have sanctioned and there should not be opposition to the action from other minority shareholders (*Smith v Croft (No 2)* [1988]). See also *Smith v Croft* [1986]; *McDonald v Horn* [1995]; *Halle v Trax Ltd* [2000].

It has been argued that of these four apparent exceptions to the rule in *Foss v Harbottle*, only the fourth is a true exception. The other three instances are said to be examples of the company violating its constitution, injuring the member, who may then pursue a personal claim against the company.

Minority protection and majority control

Statutory Derivative Claim s 260(3) CA 2006

Common Law No shareholder litigation on behalf of company – *Foss v Harbottle* [1843]

Except

1 *Ultra vires* (*Parke v Daily News Ltd*; s 539 CA 2006)

2 Special majorities (*Edwards v Halliwell*)

3 Personal rights (*Pender v Lushington*; *Wood v Odessa Waterworks*)

4 Fraud by those in control (*Cook v Deeks*; *Daniels v Daniels*; *Prudential Assurance v Newman Industries (No 2)* on 'those in control')

The other statutory remedies

Section 994 of the CA 2006

Because of difficulties with *Foss v Harbottle* a statutory remedy was introduced in s 210 of the Companies Act (CA) 1948. This followed the report of the Cohen Committee (1945). The Committee urged that:

... there be a new section under which, on a shareholder's petition, the court, if satisfied that a minority of the shareholders is being oppressed and that a winding up order would not do justice to the minority, should be empowered, instead of making a winding up order, to make such other order, including an order for the purchase by the majority of the shares of the minority at a price to be fixed by the court as to the court may seem just.

There were difficulties with s 210 of the CA 1948. These difficulties were high-lighted by the Jenkins Committee (1962). The drawbacks were as follows:

- An order could only be made if the facts could be the basis of a winding up order on the just and equitable grounds. This meant that the section was closely allied to the rules relating to winding up.

- A single act was insufficient to justify a petition under s 210 of the CA 1948. A course of conduct had to be shown.

- The petitioner had to show that the conduct was oppressive. This meant 'burdensome, harsh and wrongful' (see *Scottish Cooperative Wholesale Society v Meyer* [1959]).

- A petition could not be based on omissions or threatened future conduct.

  There was some doubt as to whether the section could be used by personal representatives, although it was stated in *Re Jermyn Street Turkish Baths Ltd* [1970] by Plowman J that personal representatives could petition.

Due to these problems (s 210 of the CA 1948 was used successfully in only two cases), the law was amended. Section 75 of the Companies Act (CA) 1980 was introduced. This is now s 994 of the CA 2006. The remedy in s 994 of the CA 2006 answered many of the difficulties of the old section. The link with winding up was swept away. A single act or an omission or threatened future conduct could be the basis for a petition, and personal representatives could sue. Most importantly, the remedy applied in cases of 'unfair prejudice'. This is clearly a far wider remedy than a remedy for oppression.

Originally the remedy was stated to be available to 'some part of the company's members'. This led to difficulties since it was interpreted in some cases as meaning that the remedy could not be used if all of the membership was unfairly prejudiced. This had been the view of Vinelott J in *Re Carrington Viyella plc* [1983], for example. The section was amended to make it clear that the remedy is available even if all of the members of the company are prejudiced. Section 994 of the CA 2006, as amended, reads as follows:

> A member of a company may apply to the court by petition for an order under this part on the ground that the company's affairs are being or have been conducted in a manner which is unfairly prejudicial to the interests of its members generally or of some part of its members (including at least himself) or that any actual or proposed act or omission of the company (including an act or omission on its behalf) is or would be so prejudicial.

The most frequent cause for complaint is exclusion from management by being removed from the board – generally in a quasi-partnership company like the one in *Ebrahimi v Westbourne Galleries Ltd* [1973]. Under the old law, it was necessary that oppression had been suffered *qua* member, so the conduct had to affect the shareholder's rights and interests, not just the person's position as director. Under s 994 of the CA 2006, the conduct complained of must be unfairly prejudicial to the interests of members in their capacity as members. A member is not entitled to complain about prejudice to some other interest (*Re A Company (No 004475 of 1982)* [1983]; *Re JE Cade and Son Ltd* [1992]), although Lord Hoffmann in *O'Neill v Phillips* [1999] thought that this requirement should not be too narrowly construed.

Petitions have been successful on the basis of exclusion in a number of cases (see *Re Bird Precision Bellows Ltd* [1986]; *Re A Company No 00477 of 1986* [1986]). In other cases, petitions on the basis of exclusion from management have failed. Where they have failed, however, this has been because of the facts.

Thus, exclusion from management failed in *Re A Company No 003843 of 1986* [1987] where the company had not been established on a quasi-partnership basis. Exclusion from management also failed in *Re A Company No 004377 of 1986 (XYZ Ltd)* [1986] where the company's constitution made provision for such an eventuality. Generally speaking, to petition successfully under s 994 of the CA 2006 for exclusion from management, the petitioner has to show that the company was formed and/or run on the basis of an understanding that the petitioner would have a role in the management of the company. Any action taken to remove the petitioner from management would then be inequitable in that it would defeat the legitimate expectations of the petitioner arising from

105

that understanding (*O'Neill v Phillips* [1999]). It is much easier to establish such legitimate expectations in the context of a quasi-partnership and virtually impossible in the context of a public company (*Re Blue Arrow plc* [1987]; *Re Astec (BSR) plc* [1998]).

It may also be that a remedy is denied where the exclusion was justified because of the petitioner's conduct (see *Re RA Noble & Sons (Clothing) Ltd* [1983]; *Woolwich v Milne* [2003]; *Larvin v Phoenix Office Supplies Ltd* [2002]).

There have been many other petitions where particular conduct has been recognised as capable of being unfairly prejudicial:

- Allotting shares in breach of pre-emption rights (*Re DR Chemicals Ltd* [1989]).

- Excessive salaries paid to the directors (*Re Cumana* [1986]).

- Convening a meeting of the company for a date unreasonably into the distant future (*McGuinness and Another, Petitioners* [1988]).

- Failure to pay proper dividends over a long period without explanation (*Re Sam Weller & Sons Ltd* [1989]).

- Diverting business away from the company (*Re London School of Electronics* [2006]).

- Making a rights issue in certain circumstances (*Re A Company No 007623 of 1984* [1986]).

- Providing misleading information to a company's shareholders (*Re A Company No 008699 of 2006* [1986]).

- A proposal to sell the company's business at a substantial undervaluation to connected persons (*Re Posgate and Denby (Agencies) Ltd* [1987]).

- Using the company's assets for the benefit of the company's controlling shareholders and family (*Re Elgindata* [1991]).

- Mismanagement of the company's affairs (but not in the sense of bad commercial decision making) (*Re Macro (Ipswich) Ltd* [1994]).

- Directors using their fiduciary powers for ulterior purposes (*Re Saul D Harrison & Sons plc* [1995]).

The section may be used by members or personal representatives of members.

106

It is not necessary that a person should come to court with clean hands (*Re London School of Electronics* [2006]). However, if a petitioner has to some extent brought the relevant conduct upon himself, this may be material in deciding whether the prejudice is unfair and it may also be relevant in deciding what remedy if any should be available to the petitioner (see *Re RA Noble & Sons (Clothing) Ltd* [1983]; *Mears v R Mears & Co (Holdings) Ltd* [2002]).

Remedies

The court has the power to award whatever relief it considers fit (s 996 of the CA 2006). It may make an order regulating the company's affairs or restricting the company from acting in a particular way. It may order the company to do something or it may order civil proceedings to be brought in the name of the company. The most common remedy is where the court orders the purchase of a petitioner's shares. On occasion, it may be an order that the respondent sells his shares to the petitioner. This occurred in *Re Brenfield Squash Racquets Club Ltd* [1996].

Where an order is made for the purchase of shares, problems of valuation arise. There is no rule in s 996 of the CA 2006 regarding a valuation of shares.

Generally, where a minority shareholding is sold, an element of discount is applied; so, for example, if 10 per cent of the shares are to be sold, this would not represent a 10 per cent value of the company's net assets. However, in relation to s 994 of the CA 2006, the sale is a forced sale. As Vinelott J said in *Re Bird Precision Bellows Ltd* [1984] at first instance:

> . . . on the assumption that the unfair prejudice has made it no longer tolerable for him to retain his interest in the company, the sale of his shares will inevitably be his only practical way out short of a winding up. In that case it seems to me that it would not merely not be fair, but most unfair that he should be bought out on a fictional basis applicable to a free election to sell his shares in accordance with the company's articles of association, or indeed on any other basis which involved a discounted price. In my judgment, the correct course would be to fix the price pro rata according to the value of the shares as a whole without any discount, as being the only fair method of compensating an unwilling vendor of the equivalent of a partnership share.

Another moot point is on what date the shares should be valued. Again, there is no fixed rule to apply. If the petitioner refused a reasonable offer for his shares, the date of valuation may well be the date of the hearing (see *Re A Company No 992567 of 1982* [1983]).

On the other hand, if a fair offer is not made and the conduct of the majority causes the value of the company's shares to fall, the court may order a valuation at the date that the unreasonable conduct began (see *Re OC (Transport) Services Ltd* [1984]). In *Profinance Trust SA v Gladstone* [2002], the Court of Appeal, after reviewing the earlier authorities, thought that the date close to when the shares are to be purchased had become the presumptive valuation date, but recognised that there may be circumstances when an earlier date might be chosen, such as where the unfairly prejudicial conduct had deprived the company of its business or there had been a general fall in the market since the presentation of the petition. Note also *O'Neill v Phillips* [1999] in relation to what constitutes a reasonable offer to purchase a petitioner's shares.

JUST AND EQUITABLE WINDING UP

It may in some ways seem incongruous to consider winding up in the context of minority remedies. In truth, however, the just and equitable ground for winding up is a member's remedy. It is important to remember this in the context of a possible essay or, indeed, a problem question relating to remedies for members.

A company may be wound up by the court if the court is of the opinion that it is just and equitable that the company should be wound up (s 122(1)(g) of the IA 1986). Before the advent of ss 994–996 of the CA 2006, just and equitable winding up was sometimes the only possible remedy for a disenchanted minority shareholder. The difficulties of framing an action as an exception to *Foss v Harbottle* have already been noted. Since the advent of ss 994–996, use of just and equitable winding up has been less common. Indeed, s 125(2) of the IA 1986 provides that if the court is of the opinion that there is some other remedy that is available to the petitioners and that they are acting unreasonably in seeking to have the company wound up instead of pursuing that other remedy, then the court should refuse the petition. However, in *Virdi v Abbey Leisure Ltd* [1990], the Court of Appeal considered that where a minority sought a winding up order, rather than utilising a mechanism in the articles for selling the shares, this was not acting unreasonably. The Court of Appeal, reversing Hoffmann J at first instance, considered that the minority might legitimately object to the mode of valuation in assessing the value of the shares and prefer to leave it to the marketplace.

The most famous case in relation to just and equitable winding up is *Ebrahimi v Westbourne Galleries Ltd* [1973]. The House of Lords in this case stated unequivocally that the categories of conduct justifying winding up on the just and equitable ground are not closed. Below you will find examples of some of the circumstances where just and equitable winding up may be awarded.

- In *Ebrahimi* itself, the ground was exclusion from management in a quasi-partnership company. This was also the ground in *Re A & BC Chewing Gum Ltd* [1975]; *Tay Bok Choon v Tahansan Sdn Bhd* [1987]; and *Re Lundie Brothers* [1965].

- Another ground on which just and equitable winding up may be awarded is where the purpose for which the company was formed can no longer be achieved (sometimes called the destruction of the substratum of the company). This was the successful ground in *Re German Date Coffee Co* [1882]. Here the company had been formed to obtain a German patent to manufacture coffee from dates. The application for the patent was refused. A petition to wind the company up was granted. Such a petition can only succeed, however, if all of the company's main purposes are no longer capable of achievement. Thus, in *Re Kitson & Co Ltd* [1946], where the company had other activities that could be accomplished in addition to the engineering business which had ceased, a petition to wind the company up was not granted.

- Where there is deadlock within the company and that deadlock cannot be broken, a petition to wind the company up will be successful. In *Re Yenidje Tobacco Co Ltd* [1916], the company had two shareholders with an equal number of shares. They were both directors. They could not agree on how the company should be run. There was no provision for breaking the deadlock and a petition to wind the company up on the just and equitable ground was therefore successful. Another example of deadlock, leading to a winding up of the company, is *Re Pioneer Ltd* [2002].

- A further ground for a just and equitable winding up petition, and one which has found favour with the courts, is lack of honesty on the part of the directors. In *Re Bleriot Manufacturing Aircraft Co* [1916], the court held that where directors had misappropriated company property, a winding up order could be made. In *Loch v John Blackwood Ltd* [1924], a Privy Council decision on appeal from the Court of Appeal of the West Indies (Barbados), where directors had failed to supply full information to the company's members, a petition was successful. Another example can be found in *Re Lundie Brothers Ltd* [1965], where directors were running the business as if it were their own personal property.

There are, therefore, certain categories of conduct which are clearly established as giving rise to the ability to present a petition to wind the company up on the just and equitable ground.

Examination questions on shareholder protection

You are advised to ensure in answering any question, whether it be an essay or a problem question, to consider the full range of shareholder protection that might be available. Sections 994–996 of the CA 2006 are extremely important. Not only will they crop up in essay and problem questions specifically designed to test a candidate's knowledge on these areas, but they must be borne in mind in answering any question on company law, as disgruntled shareholders may feature in any problem question. Make sure you are familiar with the wording of s 994 of the CA 2006. In particular, remember that a petitioner must show that there is or has been conduct of the company's affairs which is prejudicial to his interests as a member (or all of the members) and that it is unfair. Do not forget just and equitable winding up as a shareholder remedy either. In addition, there may be other areas involving shareholder protection which you may be able to use. For example, minorities are able to require company meetings to be called, and at meetings, a poll may be demanded. In short, the whole question of shareholder protection permeates the entire CA 2006 and you should seek to display a breadth of knowledge in answering examination questions involving shareholder protection.

Minority protection chief remedies – summary

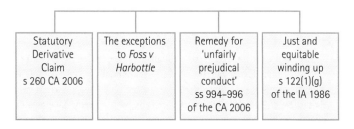

Statutory Derivative Claim s 260 CA 2006	The exceptions to *Foss v Harbottle*	Remedy for 'unfairly prejudical conduct' ss 994–996 of the CA 2006	Just and equitable winding up s 122(1)(g) of the IA 1986

COMPANY INVESTIGATIONS

PRODUCTION OF DOCUMENTS

The Department of Trade and Industry may require a company to produce documents (s 447 of the CA 1985). This power is reinforced by a power of entry and search (s 448 of the CA 1985). This is often the precursor to an investigation.

INVESTIGATION OF AFFAIRS OF A COMPANY

Section 431 of the CA 1985 provides that the Secretary of State may appoint inspectors to investigate a company's affairs on the application of not fewer than 200 members or of members holding not less than 10 per cent of the issued shares or, in the case of a company without share capital, one fifth of the members or the company itself. The application must be supported by such evidence as the Secretary of State may require.

Section 432 of the CA 1985 provides that the Secretary of State must appoint inspectors if so ordered by the court and may do so if there are circumstances suggesting:

- that the company's affairs are being or have been conducted with intent to defraud creditors or otherwise for a fraudulent or unlawful purpose or in a manner which is unfairly prejudicial to some part of the members; or

- that an actual or proposed act or omission is or would be so prejudicial or that the company was formed for any fraudulent or unlawful purpose; or

- that persons connected with the company's formation or management have been guilty of fraud, misfeasance or other misconduct toward the company or its members; or that the company's members have not been given all the information with respect to the company's affairs which they might reasonably expect (s 432(2) of the CA 1985).

Sections 1035–1039 of the CA 2006 extend the powers of the Secretary of State so that directions can be given regarding the inspection, inspectors being removed or replaced and with regard to obtaining information.

These provisions are only used in the most serious cases, see eg the investigations into House of Fraser Holdings plc, Barlow Clowes Gilt Ltd and Mirror Group Newspapers plc. Investigations tend to be lengthy and expensive. The investigation into Mirror Group Newspapers took nine years and cost £9.5m, while the Barlow Clowes investigation cost £6.25m.

INVESTIGATION OF OWNERSHIP OR CONTROL

Section 442 of the CA 1985 enables the Secretary of State to appoint inspectors if he feels there is good reason to investigate the ownership or control of a company. He must order an investigation if an application is made by 200 or more members or by members holding 10 per cent or more of the company's issued shares.

INVESTIGATION OF DIRECTORS' SHARE DEALINGS

Section 446 of the CA 1985 provides that the Secretary of State may appoint inspectors if he feels there has been a contravention of s 323 of the CA 1985 (prohibition on directors dealing in share options) or of s 324 (disclosure of directors' shareholdings).

OTHER COMPANIES IN GROUPS OF COMPANIES

In each of the above instances, the inspector may investigate any other company in a group of companies.

INVESTIGATION INTO INSIDER DEALING

Under s 168 of the Financial Services and Markets Act 2000, the Secretary of State and the Financial Services Authority can order an investigation into suspected breaches of insider dealing legislation.

CONSEQUENCES OF AN INSPECTION

An inspection may lead to:

- a petition by the Secretary of State under s 124(4) of the IA 1986 to wind the company up on the just and equitable ground (see *Re Sentinel Securities plc* [1996]; *Re Market Wizard Systems (UK) Ltd* [1998]; *Re Delfin International (SA) Ltd* [2000]);

- civil proceedings being brought by the Secretary of State in the name of the company (s 438 of the CA 1985);

- a petition being brought by the Secretary of State on the basis of unfair prejudice to the members (s 995 of the CA 2006);

- an application for a disqualification order against individual directors or shadow directors (s 8 of the Company Directors Disqualification Act 1986).

Different types of company investigation – summary

- Investigation of affairs of a company
- Investigation of ownership or control
- Investigation of directors' share dealings
- Investigation into insider dealing

You should now be confident that you would be able to tick all of the boxes on the checklist at the beginning of this chapter. To check your knowledge of Shareholder protection why not visit the companion website and take the Multiple Choice Question test. Check your understanding of the terms and vocabulary used in this chapter with the flashcard glossary.

7

The company in trouble, reconstructions and takeovers

Wrongful trading

Takeovers, reconstructions and amalgamations

Schemes of arrangement

Amalgamation

Takeovers

INTRODUCTION

This chapter covers a great deal of ground. Wrongful trading is important and topical, and knowledge of priorities in a winding up is of great importance. The changes to charges take effect from 2009.

LOAN STOCK (DEBENTURES)

Any form of borrowing by a company is technically a debenture (s 738 of the Companies Act (CA) 2006). In practice, the word 'debenture' is generally used to describe a secured borrowing and debentures are generally subject to the law of mortgages. The only exception to this principle is that a debenture need not be redeemable at a set date (s 739 of the CA 2006).

Where a company borrows money from a bank, there may be a single debenture. In other situations, particularly in relation to quoted companies, there may be an issue of debenture stock similar to an issue of shares. In such a situation, there will be a debenture trust deed. This will set out the terms of the loan. There will be a trustee who will act on behalf of all debenture holders.

DEBENTURES COMPARED WITH SHARES

Debentures and shares have certain similarities. The transfer procedure is similar. Where debentures are issued to the public, the same principles apply as in relation to an issue of shares pertaining to a prospectus or listing particulars.

Shares compared with debentures

Similarities	Distinctions
• Transfer • Issues to the public	• Debenture holder is a creditor • Shareholder is a member • Company can purchase its own debentures • Company cannot purchase its own shares (in general) • Debentures may be issued at a discount • Shares cannot be issued at a discount

Charges

It has been noted that in practice a debenture is a secured loan. A debenture may be secured in one of two ways: by a fixed charge or by a floating charge. A fixed charge is similar to an ordinary mortgage and is effective from the time of its creation.

Shares compared with debentures

The floating charge is unique to company law. It can be created over the whole of the company's assets and undertaking. It is not effective until something happens to cause the charge to crystallise. It is beneficial to the company, in that it enables the company to borrow money and to mortgage back to the lender of the money all of the company's assets and undertakings, including work in progress, finished products and raw materials. There is no statutory definition of a floating charge and what label the parties use in relation to the charge is not conclusive (see *Re ASRS Establishment Ltd* [2000]; *Agnew v Commissioner of Inland Revenue* [2001]). The nature of a floating charge was described in *Re Yorkshire Woolcombers Association Ltd* [1904], where Romer LJ stated that the floating charge is over a class of assets present and future, that the company can continue to do business and to dispose of its assets in the course of that business, and that the assets within the class of assets subject to the floating charge will fluctuate and change as the company trades.

A floating charge will crystallise in the following circumstances:

- if the company goes into liquidation;

- if a receiver is appointed, either by the court or under the terms of the debenture;

- if there is cessation of the company's trade or business;

- if an event occurs which, by the terms of the debenture, causes the floating charge to crystallise.

This last head has caused some controversy, because an issue arises as to whether a charge can crystallise simply on the happening of some event or by the giving of notice by the charge holder, as provided for by the terms of the debenture. Despite opposing views from Commonwealth decisions, it appears reasonably well settled that crystallisation can occur automatically (see the *obiter* of Hoffman J in *Re Brightlife Ltd* [1986]).

Statutory recognition of automatic crystallisation is still awaited.

Most charges require registration. Categories of charges that have to be registered are set out in s 860(7) of the CA 2006. The categories include all floating charges and most fixed charges.

The charge must be registered within 21 days of its creation. Failure to register a charge renders it void (s 874 of the CA 2006). This does not, of course, affect the validity of the debt (s 874(3) of the CA 2006). If a company acquires property that is already subject to a charge, the obligation to register accrues on the date of its acquisition. The failure to register in such a situation, however, does not render the charge void but merely exposes the officers concerned to liability to a default fine (s 860 of the CA 2006).

When a charge is paid off, a memorandum should be delivered to the registrar of companies to record this event (s 872 of the CA 2006).

A company is also obliged to keep a register of charges at its registered office (s 876 of the CA 2006). This is to be made available for inspection by any creditor or member of the company (s 877(4) of the CA 2006) and by any other person on payment of a fee (s 877(4) of the CA 2006).

Crystallisation of a floating charge

- Company goes into liquidation
- A receiver is appointed
- Company ceases to do business
- An event occurs or notice is given by the debenture holder which, under the terms of the debenture, causes crystallisation

Priorities amongst charges

Sometimes, problems may arise regarding the priority amongst various charges. This may occur where there is an administrative receivership or where there is a liquidation.

The general rule is that fixed charges which are effective from the time of creation have priority over floating charges which only have efficacy from the time of crystallisation.

The only exception to this is that a floating charge which contains a negative pledge provision may have priority over a later fixed charge. This is the principle in *Wilson v Kelland* [1910]. At present, this type of negative pledge provision is only effective if its existence is actually known by the subsequent fixed charge holder.

As between two or more fixed charges over the same property, clearly, the first in time has priority. The same principle generally applies where there is a second floating charge over the same property (see *Re Benjamin Cope & Sons Ltd* [1914]). An exception to this, however, is if the first floating charge leaves open the possibility of a second floating charge taking priority over it where the second floating charge is over a specific category of property narrower than the first which would be over the entire assets and undertaking of the company (see *Re Automatic Bottlemakers* [1926]).

In any problem concerning priorities, it is important to bear other factors in mind. Where questions of priority arise, the costs (including remuneration) of the administrative receiver or liquidator will always be paid off before fixed and floating charges. Preferential creditors are paid off ahead of the beneficiaries of a floating charge. The categories of preferential creditor are set out in Sched 6 to the *Insolvency Act (IA) 1986*.

Another important feature to bear in mind is the possibility of a valid reservation of title clause (see *Aluminium Industrie Vaassen BV v Romalpa Aluminium Ltd* [1976]). Where there is an effective reservation of title clause, this may well mean that property which is on the premises of the company concerned does not come within the control of the administrative receiver or liquidator because it still belongs to the supplier.

Consider also the position of a person holding a lien over some part of the company's property. For example, if the fleet of company cars is out for repair at a garage and the repair work has been done but the cars are still parked on the forecourt of the garage, the liquidator or administrative receiver cannot take control of the cars until he has paid the fees owing to the garage (see *George Barker (Transport) Ltd v Eynon* [1974]).

120

RECEIVERSHIP

Where a debenture holder seeks to enforce the terms of a debenture where there has been default, the appropriate remedy is generally to secure the appointment of a receiver. If the debenture holder is seeking to enforce a fixed charge, he will appoint a receiver. Such a person need not be a qualified insolvency practitioner. If he is seeking to enforce the terms of a floating charge, then he will seek to appoint an administrative receiver. Such a person must be a qualified insolvency practitioner. Members of certain professional bodies may act as insolvency practitioners. These bodies are:

- the Law Society;
- the Institute of Chartered Accountants in England and Wales;
- the Chartered Association of Certified Accountants;
- the Insolvency Practitioners Association.

Where a person is appointed as an administrative receiver, the appointment will be in writing unless it is by court order.

The person appointed as administrative receiver must notify the company of his appointment and all of the company's creditors so far as their addresses are known to him. Additionally, administrative receivers must ensure there is a statement of their appointment contained in the *London Gazette*.

In every receivership, publicity must be given to the fact that there is a receivership. It must be stated on every invoice, order for goods or business letter issued by or on behalf of the company or the receiver or manager where the company's name appears. The administrative receiver should seek to take control of the assets subject to the floating charge, realise the assets and pay off the creditors in due order of priority. As has been noted above, preferential creditors must be paid ahead of the beneficiaries of a floating charge.

The administrative receiver will require the directors of the company to produce a statement of affairs of the company setting out the company's assets, debts, liabilities and securities. The administrative receiver should draft his own report which should be sent to the registrar of companies, to any trustees for secured creditors and to all secured creditors for whom he has an address.

In general, similar principles apply in relation to a receiver where there is a fixed charge. In this situation, however, preferential creditors do not enjoy the same priority and there is no statement of affairs.

An administrative receiver may at any time be removed from office by order of the court. An administrative receiver may also resign his office and he must vacate office if he ceases to be qualified as an insolvency practitioner. Where an administrative receiver vacates office otherwise than by death, he must, within 14 days of his vacation of office, send a notice to that effect to the registrar of companies.

Under the IA 1986 (as amended by the Enterprise Act 2002), the right to appoint an administrative receiver is restricted. This is to encourage those creditors holding floating charges, particularly the banks, to opt for administration as a preferred insolvency procedure rather than receivership; although where the provisions do not apply, receivership, as an insolvency procedure, can still operate. The changes brought about by the Enterprise Act 2002 apply only to floating charges created after 15 September 2003 and not to floating charges created before this date.

VOLUNTARY ARRANGEMENTS

Voluntary arrangements are dealt with in Part 1 of the IA 1986. This provides a simple procedure where a company in financial difficulties can enter into a voluntary arrangement with its creditors. It may involve a composition in satisfaction of debts or a scheme of arrangement of the company's affairs.

The voluntary arrangement must be supervised by a 'nominee'. This nominee must be a qualified insolvency practitioner. The nominee should submit a report to the court stating whether in his opinion meetings of the company and of its creditors should be summoned to consider the proposal put to him by directors of the company. The proposal where meetings are called must be approved by three quarters in value of the creditors and by a simple majority of the members.

Once the proposal for the voluntary arrangement has taken effect, the nominee becomes the supervisor of the composition or of the scheme of arrangement.

To avoid the possibility of a creditor taking individual action while a voluntary arrangement is being considered, such as seeking the appointment of a receiver, under IA 2000, a small company will be able to obtain a moratorium on creditor action while a proposal for a voluntary arrangement is being considered. As indicated below, obtaining an administration order is an alternative method of avoiding similar creditor action, but administration can be expensive. However, a moratorium cannot be obtained until there is a viable proposal for a voluntary arrangement and a nominee has agreed to act. The effects on the company's creditors of a moratorium are similar to the effects of an administration order.

ADMINISTRATION

Administration is an insolvency procedure which was introduced following a recommendation of the Cork Committee (1981).

The IA 1986 provides for the rescue of a company by placing its management in the hands of an administrator. The administrator must be a qualified insolvency practitioner.

The court may make an administration order on the application, *inter alia*, of the company, its directors, one or more creditors of the company, or the supervisor of a voluntary arrangement. Under the changes introduced by the Enterprise Act 2002, it is possible for an administrator to be appointed out of court, by either the company's floating charge holders, who, in relation to charges created after 15 September 2003, will no longer be able to appoint an administrative receiver, the company itself, or the directors of the company, subject to certain conditions being met. There are some exceptions to these provisions, which are inserted into the IA 1986, with effect from 15 September 2003.

Before 15 September 2003, for an administration order to be granted, the court had to be satisfied that the company was unable, or was likely to become unable, to pay its debts and that the making of an order would make one or more of the following purposes achievable:

- the survival of the company as a going concern in whole or in part;

- the approval of a voluntary arrangement under Part 1 of the IA (see above);

- the sanctioning of a scheme of arrangement under s 895 of the CA 2006 between the company and such persons as are mentioned in that section;

- a more advantageous realisation of the company's assets than would be effected on a winding up.

The amended provisions of the IA 1986 require any administrator to act in the interests of the creditors as a whole and, in so doing, to pursue the following objectives in the following order of priority:

1 rescuing the company as a going concern;
2 achieving a better result for the creditors as a whole than would be likely if the company were wound up;
3 realising property in order to make a distribution to one or more secured or preferential creditors, so long as in so doing he does not unnecessarily harm the interests of the other creditors of the company as a whole.

Where a company is in administration, none of the following may occur:

- no resolution may be passed or order made to wind the company up (except a compulsory winding up on public interest petitions);

- no steps can be taken to enforce any security of the company's property or to repossess goods in the company's possession under any hire purchase agreement (this includes leasing agreements and retention of title agreements) except with the consent of the administrator or the permission of the court;

- no other proceedings and no execution or other legal process may be commenced or continued and no distress levied against the company or its property except with the consent of the administrator or the permission of the court.

Where the court gives permission, it may impose a condition on the transaction or a requirement in connection with the transaction. The moratorium on legal action also applies from the moment an application for an administrative order is made or the notice of intention to appoint an administrator is filed. However, this interim moratorium does not stop certain specified actions.

A court cannot grant an administration order if an administrative receiver is also in office, unless the appointee of the administrative receiver consents to the administration order or the court thinks that the appointee's security may be set aside if an administration order were made. On an administration order being made, an administrative receiver must vacate office and a receiver must do so if requested by the administrator. An administration order cannot be made and neither can an administrator be appointed if the company is in liquidation or is already in administration, although in respect of a liquidation, the court can discharge a winding up order if an administration order is made on the application of a floating charge holder or the liquidator. In respect of the out of court procedure, an administrator cannot be appointed if an administrative receiver is in office nor, in the case of an appointment by a company or its directors, if there are any outstanding winding up petitions or applications for administration in respect of the company.

The administrator should require a statement of affairs to be made to him by those who have been running the company. He then drafts his own proposals for achieving the purpose or purposes set out in the IA 1986, laying a copy of the statement before a meeting of the company's creditors. He should also send a copy of the statement to all members of the company or publish it in the prescribed manner, setting out the address to which members should write for copies of the statement to be sent to them free of charge.

During the currency of an administration, s 27 of the IA 1986 provides that a creditor or member may apply to the court for an order on the ground that the company's affairs, business or property are being or have been managed in a manner which is unfairly prejudicial to the interests of its creditors or members generally or some part of them or that any act or proposed act or omission of the administrator is or would be so prejudicial.

The provisions in the IA 1986 relating to fair dealing, namely transactions at an undervalue (s 238), preferences (s 239), extortionate credit transactions (s 244) and the invalidity of certain floating charges (s 245), apply to administration as they apply to liquidation.

LIQUIDATION

TYPES OF LIQUIDATION

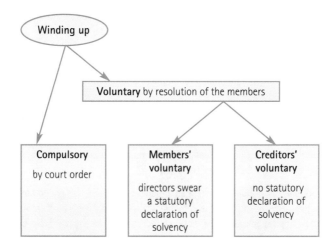

There are essentially two types of winding up. There is compulsory winding up which is by court order, and voluntary winding up which is initiated by the members of the company. Voluntary winding up may be further split into two types:

- a members' voluntary winding up, largely under the control of the members where the directors swear a statutory declaration of solvency; and

- a creditors' voluntary winding up, largely under the control of the creditors where the directors have failed to swear a statutory declaration of solvency.

Compulsory liquidation

Section 122(1) of the IA 1986 sets out the various grounds for compulsory winding up. They are as follows:

- the company has by special resolution resolved that the company be wound up by the court;

- the company is a public company which is registered as such on initial incorporation but has not been issued with a certificate to do business under s 761 of the CA 2006 and more than a year has passed since it was so registered;

- the company is an old public company within the meaning of the Companies (Consequential Provisions) Act 1985;

- the company has not commenced business within a year of incorporation or suspends business for a year;

- the number of members is reduced to below two, unless it is a private company to which the exemption relating to membership of one applies;

- the company is unable to pay its debts;

- the court is of the opinion that it is just and equitable that the company should be wound up.

The last two grounds are the most important.

A company is unable to pay its debts if the conditions in s 123 of the IA 1986 are satisfied. Inability to pay debts is demonstrated by one of the following:

- if a creditor is owed a debt exceeding £750 for three weeks after making a written request for payment of that debt;

- execution or process issued on a judgment is returned unsatisfied in whole or in part (in practice the minimum sum owed must exceed £750);

- if it is proved to the satisfaction of the court that the company is unable to pay its debts as they fall due (in practice, the same minimum sum applies);

- if the company's assets are worth less than the amount of its liabilities, taking account of contingent and prospective liability (in practice, the same minimum sum applies).

The last ground set out in s 122 of the IA 1986 (just and equitable winding up) has been considered above.

In a compulsory winding up, if the case is made out, the petition may be granted. The commencement date of the liquidation is the date that the petition is presented, that is, retrospectively the date of the commencement of liquidation is the date of the petition. This date is important for the calculation of time limits, for example, for the fair dealing provisions of IA 1986.

Once a winding up petition has been presented, then any disposition of the company's property and any transfer of shares or alteration of its status is void unless the court orders otherwise.

Where a winding up order is granted, the court will appoint a provisional liquidator and that liquidator will be the official receiver (s 136(2) of the IA 1986).

Separate meetings of creditors and contributories will be called for the purpose of choosing a permanent liquidator. The creditors and the contributories (the members) at their respective meetings may nominate a person to be liquidator and nominate representatives to a liquidation committee. The liquidator will generally be the person nominated by the creditors in the event of a conflict. The same meetings may nominate people to a liquidation committee. The purpose of the liquidation committee will be to liaise with the liquidator during the course of a winding up.

A statement of affairs is usually required by the official receiver.

Voluntary liquidation

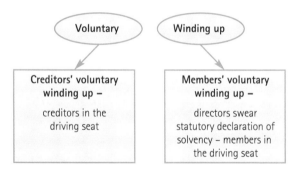

Voluntary liquidation may commence in the following ways:

- if a fixed period has been settled for the duration of the company and the fixed period has now elapsed, then the company may be wound up by ordinary resolution;

- if the company resolves to be wound up voluntarily by a special resolution;

▪ if the company resolves by extraordinary resolution to be wound up on the basis that it cannot by reason of its liabilities continue its business (s 84 of the IA 1986).

If the directors of the company or a majority of them swear to the effect that the company will be able to pay its debts in full together with interest within the next 12 months, then this represents a statutory declaration of solvency (s 89 of the IA 1986). Where there is such a declaration, the liquidation will proceed as a members' voluntary winding up. The interests of the creditors are supposedly protected by the statutory declaration of solvency.

Where this is the case, there will be a general meeting of members to pass a resolution to wind up and to appoint somebody as liquidator. In such a situation, there is no liquidation committee.

If there is no statutory declaration of solvency, then the liquidation proceeds as a creditors' voluntary winding up. Here, general meetings of contributories and creditors will be convened. Each will nominate a liquidator but if there is a conflict, the creditors' choice will prevail. Once again, there will be a liquidation committee made up of equal numbers of representatives of the creditors and of the contributories.

A statement of affairs is made by the directors.

PRIORITIES IN A LIQUIDATION

Examination questions – usually problem questions – on priorities in a liquidation arise frequently. In order to be able to tackle such questions, you should be familiar with the provisions relating to registration of charges, provisions on reservation of title clauses, the law of liens, and the fair dealing provisions of the IA 1986.

Most charges are registrable. They only enjoy priority as charges if properly registered. Failure to register does not, of course, affect the validity of the debt, merely the validity of the security. Section 860 of the CA 2006 sets out the categories of charges that are registrable. The categories include all floating charges and most fixed charges. Charges are registrable within 21 days of their creation or acquisition. Failure to register a charge created by the company within the 21 day period may mean that the charge is void against an administrator or liquidator or any person acquiring an interest in or right over property subject to the charge. However, where a company acquires property already subject to a charge, failure to register will not affect the validity of such a charge, it will only render the company and any officer in default liable to a fine.

There is provision for late delivery of particulars under s 861 of the CA 2006, by application to the court. Section 869 of the CA 2006 permits delivery of further particulars to supplement or vary the registered particulars. To the extent that registered particulars do not contain relevant information and are incomplete, then the charge is void to that extent.

In answering a question, therefore, careful consideration needs to be given as to whether or not the charge is valid. There may also be consideration of supervening invalidity under the fair dealing provisions considered below.

As between different categories of charge, floating charges rank behind fixed charges, including subsequent fixed charges. The only exception to this principle is where there is a negative pledge clause contained in the instrument creating the floating charge providing that the company cannot create any subsequent charge, fixed or floating, with priority over the floating charge. If this negative pledge provision is actually known to the subsequent charge holder, then the fixed charge will rank behind the floating charge (see *Wilson v Kelland* [1910]).

As between fixed charges over the same property, the first in point of time takes priority. As regards floating charges, where there is more than one floating charge, generally, the first floating charge will take priority over the second. This is, however, subject to an exception where the first floating charge leaves open the possibility of a subsequent floating charge taking priority and the second floating charge is over a lesser category of property than the first (see *Re Automatic Bottlemakers* [1926]).

The liquidator will need to ensure in seeking to harness the property of the company and paying off creditors in due order of priority that all of the apparent property that the company holds actually belongs to the company. In commercial practice, it is not infrequently the case that suppliers will seek to reserve title in goods until they have been fully paid for. Such reservation of title clauses take their name from the case *Aluminium Industrie Vaassen BV v Romalpa Aluminium Ltd* [1976] – and are often referred to as *Romalpa* clauses. Where a supplier reserves full title to property and creates a fiduciary relationship between the supplier and the supplied and there is no admixture of the property concerned, title to the property will remain with the supplier until the goods have been fully paid for. This was what transpired in *Romalpa* itself.

> ▶ ALUMINIUM INDUSTRIE VAASSEN BV v ROMALPA
> ALUMINIUM LTD [1976]
>
> **The claimants sold foil to the defendants. In the contract the claimant had reserved full title to property until it was paid for. The goods were delivered but the defendants went into receivership.**
>
> It was decided that the clause created a fiduciary relationship between the supplier and the supplied and as goods were kept separately, title to the property remained with the supplier until the goods were fully paid for.
>
> The clause is important for the recognition of *Romalpa* clauses.

In subsequent cases, the principle has been applied. In *Borden (UK) Ltd v Scottish Timber Products Ltd* [1980], there was a mixture of resin (in which title had been reserved) and chipboard. In such circumstances, there could be no effective reservation of title.

In *Re Bond Worth Ltd* [1980], the supplier sought only to reserve beneficial title to the goods. In such circumstances, the terms of business will necessarily imply that legal ownership has passed and, therefore, the supplier has merely created a charge which was void for non-registration, in accordance with the CA 2006.

An interesting decision on reservation of title clauses is to be found in *Hendy Lennox (Industrial Engines) Ltd v Graeme Puttick Ltd* [1984]. In this case, the supplier of diesel engines sought to reserve title to the engines. The engines were installed into generators. The court held that reservation was effective here since although the engines were installed into the generators they were not inextricably linked with them and the engines could be removed.

Another interesting example is to be found in *Armour v Thyssen AG* [1990], where the House of Lords held that an 'all-monies' clause was effective in retaining ownership in the disputed goods, even though they had been fully paid for. This was due to the nature of the clause, which provided that ownership in the goods remained with the seller while there were outstanding sums in connection with goods supplied under other contracts.

As well as difficult problems on reservation of title clauses, the examiner sometimes slips in a lien. A lien for these purposes exists where a person does work on property, for example, repairing cars or machinery. The person performing the work has a lien over the property which he has worked upon until paid for his work. Where a company goes into liquidation and property is held by somebody in such a situation, the liquidator cannot take the property until he has paid the fee (see *George Barker (Transport) Ltd v Eynon* [1974]).

Void charges

Charges may be invalid under certain provisions of the IA 1986, commonly known as the fair dealing provisions. Floating charges may, for example, be held invalid under s 245 of the IA 1986. A floating charge created in favour of a connected person within a period of two years before the onset of insolvency is invalid except to the extent that it made for good consideration or within 12 months of the insolvency if it is made in favour of an unconnected person. If it is made in favour of an unconnected person, it also needs to be demonstrated that at the time the charge was created the company was unable to pay its debts. In *Re Shoelace* [1993], the Court of Appeal considered that a floating charge came within the scope of s 245 of the IA 1986 unless the consideration for which it was made was contemporaneous (*de minimis* excepted).

Both fixed and floating charges may be caught by s 239 of the IA 1986 if they constitute a preference. A charge will constitute a preference if at the relevant time it is unfairly preferring some creditors over others. Relevant time means the period of six months ending with the onset of insolvency or, in the case of a preference in favour of a connected person, the period of two years ending with the onset of insolvency. The period concerned culminates with the onset of insolvency.

Priority of payment

In addition to the provisions on the registration of charges, reservation of title clauses, liens and the possible invalidity of charges, you should be familiar with the priority of payment.

First, the liquidator is able to claim remuneration and expenses of the liquidation. An exhaustive list of recoverable expenses is to be found in the Insolvency Rules 1986 (see *Re Toshoku Finance (UK) plc, Kahn v Inland Revenue Commissioners* [2002]; *Re Floor Fourteen Ltd, Lewis v Inland Revenue Commissioners* [2001]). Such expenses include, with effect to companies going into liquidation after 1 January 2003, expenses incurred by a liquidator in bringing proceedings in connection with s 213 of the IA 1986 (fraudulent trading), s 214 of the IA 1986 (wrongful trading), s 238 of the IA 1986 (transactions at an undervalue), s 239 of the IA 1986 (preferences) and s 423 of the IA 1986 (transactions defrauding creditors). The costs of proceedings brought under s 212 of the IA 1986 (misfeasance) or s 127 of the IA 1986 (post-petition dispositions) are not affected by the amendment, as these costs are in any event recoverable under the Insolvency Rules 1986, as being a right belonging to the company with a view to realising or restoring company assets.

The next payment is to the beneficiaries of a fixed charge, or fixed charges if there is more than one fixed charge.

Preferential creditors are paid off next. Preferential creditors are identified in Sched 6 to the IA 1986 as amended by the Enterprise Act 2002, with the different categories ranking equally. Subject to the abolition of Crown preference by the Enterprise Act 2002, with effect to new insolvencies from 15 September 2003, the types of preferential debts are as follows:

- PAYE contributions due in the 12 months before liquidation commences.

- VAT which is due for the six month period before liquidation.

- Car tax due in the 12 month period before liquidation.

- General betting duty, bingo duty and pool betting duty payable in the 12 month period before liquidation.

- NI contributions which are due for the 12 month period before liquidation.

- Any sums owing to occupational and state pension schemes.

- Wages due to employees for the four month period before liquidation up to £800 per employee.

▓ Any accrued holiday pay owed to employees.

▓ Levies on coal and steel production (derived from EU law).

Under the Employment Rights Act 1996, where, on application by the employee, the Secretary of State pays certain amounts due to the employee, he is subrogated to the employee's position in the employer's insolvency, including the employee's preferential rights. However, the Secretary of State's further right under the Employment Rights Act 1996 to be paid before employees of the insolvent employer, becomes lost under Sched B1 to the IA 1986, as from 15 September 2003.

After the preferential creditors have been paid off, the beneficiaries of floating charges are paid off next. However, in respect of new insolvencies from 15 September 2003, under s 176A of the IA 1986 (as inserted by the Enterprise Act 2002), the Secretary of State can, by order, prescribe a part of the property which would otherwise be payable to floating charge holders to be reserved for unsecured creditors. The rule can be disapplied in respect of a scheme of arrangement or a voluntary arrangement. The amount to be set aside depends on the value of the company's net property, as follows:

▓ Where the company's net property (after the payment of the costs of liquidation and the preferential creditors) does not exceed £10,000 in value, the amount to be set aside is 50 per cent.

▓ However, the liquidator does not have to distribute the funds to the unsecured creditors if he considers that this would be disproportionate to the costs involved.

▓ Where the company's net property exceeds £10,000, the amount to be set aside is 50 per cent of the first £10,000 and 20 per cent of the remainder, with a ceiling of £600,000.

A change made by the CA 2006 is that unsecured creditors can be paid in priority to floating charge holders (s 176ZA IA 1986). Within this category would be any person who has a preferential claim but whose preferential claim does not extend to all of the debt, for example, an employee who is owed £1,000 back salary (£200 would be non-preferential). The category would include also secured creditors in respect of the balance of any claim that was not covered by the value of the security.

After unsecured creditors (including ordinary trade creditors) are paid off, deferred creditors are paid off. The only important category of a deferred debt is a dividend which has been declared but not paid.

After this, if there is a surplus of assets (which may well be the case as many liquidations are solvent ones), then capital is returned to members in accordance with their class rights.

FAIR DEALING PROVISIONS

In any liquidation and, as has been seen, in an administration, the fair dealing provisions of IA 1986 are of importance.

Section 238 of the IA 1986 provides that an administrator or liquidator may apply to the court for an order of restitution where the company has entered into a transaction at an undervalue, where the company makes a gift or receives significantly less consideration for a property than its true value. An order may be made if the transaction is in favour of a connected person within two years of the onset of insolvency, or if in favour of an unconnected person within six months of the onset of insolvency (this will be the date of the presentation of the petition if it is a compulsory winding up, or the date of the resolution if it is a voluntary winding up or the date of presentation of the petition to appoint an administrator in this case).

The same principle applies in relation to preferences (s 239 of the IA 1986). Preferring some creditors to others in the period before insolvency will constitute a preference. Thus, in *Re M Kushler Ltd* [1943], where a bank overdraft was paid off releasing a director's guarantee before liquidation, this was challenged under the old law where similar principles applied. This was successful.

Extortionate credit transactions, where creditors supply to the company on terms where the payments are grossly exorbitant or where the terms otherwise grossly contravene ordinary principles of fair dealing, are caught by s 244 of the IA 1986. Here, the time limit is a three year period terminating with the date of the administration order or the date when the liquidation commenced.

Section 245 of the IA 1986 renders certain floating charges void. A floating charge created in favour of a connected person within the two years before the onset of insolvency is invalid except to the extent that it is made for good consideration or within 12 months of the onset of insolvency if it is made in favour of an unconnected person. If it is made in favour of an unconnected person, it needs to be shown that at the time the charge was created, the company was unable to pay its debts.

Transactions which defraud creditors under s 423 of the IA 1986 and post-petition dispositions under s 127 of the IA 1986 can also be attacked.

MISFEASANCE

Another important area in relation to liquidation concerns penalisation of directors and officers for misfeasance under s 212 of the IA 1986. This covers the situation where the person who has been an officer, liquidator, administrator or administrative receiver or concerned in the promotion, formation or management of the company has misapplied or retained or become accountable for the company's money or property or has been guilty of any misfeasance or breach of any fiduciary or other duty in relation to the company.

Fraudulent trading

Section 213 of the IA 1986 provides that the court may make an order against a person to make a contribution to the company's assets where that person has used the company to trade fraudulently. Actual deceit must be proved but the section is not limited to officers of the company.

The section provides that if, in the course of the winding up, it appears that any business of the company has been carried on with intent to defraud creditors of the company or creditors of any other person, or for any fraudulent purpose, then the liquidator can apply to the court for a declaration that any persons who were knowingly parties to the carrying on of the business in this way be liable to make such contributions to the company's assets as the court thinks proper. The words 'defraud' and 'fraudulent purpose' in the section are words which refer to 'actual dishonesty, involving, according to current notions of fair trading among commercial men, real moral blame' (*Re Patrick and Lyon Ltd* [1933]; *Bernasconi v Nicholas Bennett & Co* [2000]).

Wrongful trading

Section 214 of the IA 1986 extends liability to directors or shadow directors who should know, or ought to have concluded, that there was no reasonable prospect that the company would avoid going into insolvent liquidation. The previous law only penalised fraudulent trading where a person trading through the medium of the company actually knew that the company could not pay its debts. Section 214 of the IA 1986 therefore extends liability to the situation where a person ought to have realised that the company could not pay its debts. The section is, however, limited to directors and shadow directors. Furthermore, there is no criminal provision as there is for fraudulent trading (s 993 of the CA 2006).

There are various reasons why claims for wrongful trading might be rare. First, it may not be easy to prove that a director ought to have known of the company's insolvency. Secondly, directors of companies may often themselves be in financial difficulty making it pointless for liquidators to pursue them. Thirdly, the uncertainty of a claim may be such that a liquidator is unwilling to risk company assets in pursuing a wrongful trading claim.

Significantly, wrongful trading is based upon an objective standard. Previously, directors' duties have tended to be a matter of subjective judgment (see *Re City Equitable Fire Insurance Co Ltd* [1925]).

The section was considered in *Re Produce Marketing Consortium Ltd (No 2)* [1989]. In this case, the liquidator of the company sought an order under s 214 of the IA 1986 against two directors. The auditors of the company which was in the business of importing fruit had warned the directors of the company's serious financial position. The judge found the directors liable to contribute £75,000. In determining how to decide whether the directors ought to have known of the company's position, Knox J had this to say:

> The knowledge to be imputed in testing whether or not directors knew or ought to have concluded that there was no reasonable prospect of the company avoiding insolvent liquidation is not limited to the documentary material actually available at the given time. This appears from s 214(4) which includes a reference to facts which a director of a company not only should know but those which he ought to ascertain, a word which does not appear in s 214(2)(b). In my judgment, this indicates that there is to be included by way of factual information not only what was actually there, but what, given reasonable diligence and an appropriate level of general knowledge, skill and experience, was ascertainable.

In *Re Purpoint Ltd* [1991], Vinelott J held a director of the company liable under the wrongful trading section where it should have been plain to him that the company could not avoid going into insolvent liquidation.

It has been suggested that banks which advance money to companies and then give directions to companies as to how to run their affairs where the companies are in financial difficulties may risk being held liable under the section. In *Re MC Bacon* [1990], a liquidator brought an action against a bank for wrongful trading as a shadow director. A shadow director is defined in s 250 of the CA 2006 as:

> . . . a person in accordance with whose directions or instructions the directors of the company are accustomed to act. However, a person is not deemed a shadow director by reason only that the directors act on advice given by him in a professional capacity.

On consideration of the matter as a preliminary issue, Knox J refused to strike out a claim against the bank. He held that the claim could proceed. The matter did not proceed to trial but at the full trial Millett J considered the claim against the bank had been properly dropped.

In *Re Hydrodam (Corby) Ltd* [1994], the question of wrongful trading once again appeared before Millett J. The company was a wholly owned subsidiary of Eagle Trust plc. The liquidator alleged that Eagle Trust, a subsidiary of Eagle Trust and the directors of Eagle Trust were liable for wrongful trading. Millett J accepted that, although the company had no active directors (although some directors were appointed), Eagle Trust could be a shadow director of the company. He held, however, that it did not follow that the directors of Eagle Trust were also shadow directors of the company. This would only be the case if the directors of Eagle Trust, who owed their duties to Eagle Trust, were in the practice of giving directions and instructions to the company which the company's directors acted upon. Millett J held that the case had not been made out in the case before him.

For the other case on shadow directors, see *Kuwait Asia Bank EC v National Mutual Life Nominees Ltd* [1991]; *Re Unisoft Group Ltd (No 3)* [1994]; *Secretary of State for Trade and Industry v Deverell* [2000].

Developments in wrongful trading are clearly important, not just for questions on insolvency, but also in relation to questions of breaches of directors' duties.

Section 214 of the IA 1986 has been used, for example, by Hoffmann J in *Norman v Theodore Goddard* [1991], in developing an objective standard of care and skill for directors. It was also employed by the same judge, sitting as Hoffmann LJ, in *Re D'Jan of London Ltd* [1994].

TAKEOVERS, RECONSTRUCTIONS AND AMALGAMATIONS

SCHEMES OF ARRANGEMENT

Sections 895–899 CA 2006 provide for schemes of arrangement. A scheme of arrangement would be made between the company and its creditors or members. The provisions are usually utilised where there is an internal reconstruction. The procedure involves application to the court with the proposed plan. If the proposed plan is legal, then the court will order meetings of the members and creditors as appropriate. If the meetings give the required consent by 75 per cent in value of shares or debts, then this is reported back to the court which will then sanction the scheme if satisfied that the required consent is given. This procedure is relatively costly.

AMALGAMATION

A procedure for merger is offered somewhat incongruously by the IA 1986 where a company goes into voluntary liquidation, the liquidator may accept shares from a transferee company in exchange for assets of the company. The shares of the transferee company are then distributed to the former members of the transferor company. One drawback with the procedure is that a dissentient member of the transferor company can insist on his interest being purchased for cash.

TAKEOVERS

The law has been restated in accordance with the EU directive on Takeover Bids [2004]. The Code on Takeovers and Mergers has been placed within a statutory framework. Sections 942–946 of the CA 2006 give the Panel on Takeovers and Mergers wide powers and responsibilities. The courts will be able to judicially review the actions of the Panel. The jurisdiction of the Panel has been extended to cover all takeover bids within the Takeover Directive with a UK element.

Some of the key changes include a requirement for director's reports to contain detailed information on the share and management structures of the company (s 992 CA 2006); the new offence relating to bid documentation (s 953 CA 2006); changes to the compulsory purchase of shares if there is takeover offer (Part 28, Chapter 2 of the CA 2006) and s 966 CA 2006 which applies to pre-bid defences.

Sections 974–991 CA 2006 provide for the compulsory acquisition of shares where the offeror acquires 90 per cent of the shares of a target company. The acquisition of the minority holding will be ordered on the same terms as the majority was acquired. Not only does the majority have a right to acquire the minority, but the minority has a corresponding right to be acquired.

You should now be confident that you would be able to tick all of the boxes on the checklist at the beginning of this chapter. To check your knowledge of The company in trouble, reconstructions and takeovers why not visit the companion website and take the Multiple Choice Question test. Check your understanding of the terms and vocabulary used in this chapter with the flashcard glossary.

8

Putting it into practice ...

Now that you've mastered the basics, you will want to put it all into practice. The Routledge Questions and Answers series provides an ideal opportunity for you to apply your understanding and knowledge of the law and to hone your essay-writing technique.

We've included one exam-style essay question, which replicates the type of questions posed in Routledge Questions and Answers series to give you some essential exam practice. The Q&A includes an answer plan and a fully worked model answer to help you recognise what examiners might look for in your answer.

QUESTION 1

Do the advantages of incorporation compensate for the bureaucracy involved in running a company?

Checklist

Students should be familiar with:

- how a company can be formed and the differing types of company;
- advantages and disadvantages of incorporation;
- effects of incorporation;
- circumstances in which the separate legal personality of a company can be disregarded, both at common law and by statute (particularly fraudulent and wrongful trading);
- promoters, particularly their duties and rights;
- liability for pre-incorporation contracts.

Students should be aware that related issues which could be linked to questions based on this area include:

- the distribution of power within a company;
- enforcement of the articles of association;
- liability and/or protection of directors/investors, including disqualification of directors;
- restructuring of share capital.

Answer plan

A question such as this – a variant on the very well-worked theme of the advantages and disadvantages of incorporation – can only be tackled by someone who knows the material. It is very difficult to score high marks on such a question, since there is little scope for anything but a neat summary of the advantages of incorporation and a further summary of the bureaucratic requirements alluded to – a rare question where a list might be beneficial. It should be noted, however, that the wise student does not comment on the dullness of the question.

ANSWER

Incorporation of an existing or projected enterprise (not necessarily a business) can be achieved either by forming a company in compliance with the procedures laid down in the Companies Act (CA) 2006 or by buying a pre-existing company 'off-the-shelf' (the latter procedure accounts for about 60% of 'formations'). In either case, to incorporate a company, s 9 CA 2006 requires the delivery, to the registrar of companies, of a memorandum of association (s 8 CA 2006), an application for registration (ss 9–12 CA 2006) and a statement of compliance (s 13 CA 2006). Articles of association are also required to be registered, by virtue of s 18 CA 2006. The content of the articles, which are the company's internal rules, are determined by the founders of the company. If articles are not registered or the articles that are registered do not exclude or modify the 'default' articles of CA 2006 for different types of companies will apply (s 20 CA 2006). Previously, the default articles were Table A of the CA 1985 if the company was limited by shares. The advantage of purchasing an off-the-shelf company is that the company already exists and there is no delay between deciding to form a company and the company coming into existence through the registration process; there is merely a transfer of shareholding. This obviates the problem of pre-incorporation contracts and the possibility of having stationery printed bearing a name which, by the time the company is registered, has been taken by another company. However, an off-the-shelf company would not have been formed with the specific requirements of the promoters in mind and alterations of the memorandum or articles might be required. Indeed, problems can arise when the new shareholders of the company fail to make the necessary amendments. For example, in *Re A Company (No 005287 of 1985)* [1986], a 'shareholder' who wished to use s 994 CA 2006 (previously s 459 CA 1985) to bring an action against his fellow 'shareholders'

143

was denied *locus standi* when it was discovered that the shares in the company, which had been purchased off-the-shelf, had never been transferred to the purchasers. For most people interested in forming (or buying) a company, the appropriate form of company will be a private company limited by shares (ss 3(1), 3(2) & 4(1) CA 2006).

The UK has traditionally had more companies than other European countries of comparable size (there are almost one and a half million at present). What are the attractions of incorporation? The principal advantage of incorporation, from which a variety of benefits flow, is that a company is a distinct legal entity with rights and duties independent of those possessed by its shareholders, directors and employees — it is a legal person. In consequence, for example, business conducted in the name of a registered company is separate from the personal affairs of the human beings who act for the company, and separate also from the affairs of any other business that those human beings may conduct on behalf of another registered company. Corporate personality was created by statute in the first half of the nineteenth century, but the full significance of this provision was not appreciated until the famous case of *Salomon v Salomon & Co Ltd* [1897].

In *Salomon*, S converted his existing, successful business into a limited company, of which he was the managing director. S valued his business at £39,000 (an honest but optimistic valuation) and received from the company, in discharge of this sum, a cash amount, a debenture (an acknowledgement of debt) and 20,001 £1 shares out of the issued share capital of £20,007. S's wife and five children each held one of the remaining issued shares (seven being the minimum number of shareholders at that date), probably as his nominee. The company went into insolvent liquidation within a year with no assets to pay off the unsecured creditors. The issue for the courts was whether S was liable for the company's unpaid debts. The House of Lords, reversing the Court of Appeal, held that the company had been properly formed and was a legal person in its own right, separate from S, notwithstanding his dominant position within the company. The company was not S's agent and, consequently, S's liability was to be determined solely by reference to the Companies Act 1862. The Act required a shareholder to contribute to the debts of a company only where he held shares in respect of which the full nominal value had not been paid. S had paid for his shares in full by transferring the business to the company, so he had no liability to the creditors of the company. Thus, the *Salomon* case established that legal personality would be recognised even when one shareholder effectively controlled the company and had fixed the value of the assets used to pay for his shares.

The effects of separate legal personality are many and include the following:

▨ a company can sue and be sued in its own name;

▨ a company has perpetual succession. A company cannot die simply because all its shareholders are dead, although it can be wound up or struck off the Register by the Registrar of Companies if it appears to be moribund. Because a company exists unless and until it is wound up or deregistered, property, once transferred to the company, remains the property of the company, to do with as it pleases. There are no death duties to pay on the property because the company does not die and no costs are incurred in transferring the legal title to the property on a change of shareholder or director;

▨ the shareholders, directors and employees are not liable for criminal or tortious acts committed by the company, although they may incur personal liability concurrent with that of the company. For example, a company might, through the combined acts or omissions of several employees, establish and operate an unsafe system of work which caused the death of an employee. The company would be liable but an individual director or employee would not be liable unless he was personally negligent or the company was acting as an agent or employee of that individual;

▨ the shareholders, directors and employees are not liable on (nor can they enforce) contracts entered into by the company. As with criminal and tortious liability, an individual may incur personal liability concurrent with that of the company if he also enters into the contract. Furthermore, when the company acts as the agent of a shareholder or director (or an employee, but this is a rare event), the individual is liable under the normal rules of agency;

▨ a company may be formed with limited liability (s 3(1) CA 2006). Limited liability allows the members of a company to limit their responsibility for a company's debts. Liability may be limited to a predetermined sum, payable on winding up (a company limited by guarantee—s 3(3) CA 2006), or to the nominal value of the shares held, unless this sum has been paid by the current or a former shareholder (a company limited by shares — s 3(2)

CA 2006). Since most shares are issued fully paid, shareholders have, effectively, no liability for the company's debts;

▪ where a company has transferable shares, ownership of the company can be split or transferred without affecting the company itself;

▪ formation of a company may bring financial benefits. For example, a company can raise money to create floating charges and, perhaps, to minimise the tax liability of shareholders.

There are drawbacks to separate legal personality, in that the property of the company, not being that of the members, cannot be insured by a member and the company cannot claim on an insurance effected by a person on property which he then owned but subsequently transferred to the company (see *Macaura v Northern Assurance Co. Ltd* [1925]). Moreover, the assets of the company are the property of the company and a shareholder, even a controlling shareholder, cannot simply help himself to the company's cash. In addition, there is a limited number of situations where Parliament or the courts have decreed that corporate personality should be ignored. For example, where the directors have engaged in fraudulent or wrongful trading, they can incur personal liability (ss 213 & 214 of the Insolvency Act (IA) 1986). Sections 82–84 CA 2006 imposes liability upon an officer of the company who fails to disclose the name of the company, etc on specified documentation or at a specified location as prescribed by regulations. But what bureaucratic drawbacks are there to incorporation? In return for the advantages of incorporation, Parliament requires the observation of mandatory rules on the operation of a company. These rules are lengthy and complex and there can be no doubt that, in most companies, many administrative rules, for example on the conduct of meetings, are largely ignored. Perhaps in recognition of the widespread lack of use of some of the rules, the government has sought to reduce the administrative burden on companies, especially smaller companies, by the passing of the CA 2006. The CA 2006 permits a private company to dispense with the holding of annual general meetings and to pass written resolutions by a bare or three quarters' majority.

Such reforms are small measures, and even with the passing of the Companies Act 2006 on certain administrative aspects of the formation and running of companies, there is still an immense amount of law imposing obligations upon companies, shareholders and directors which would not apply to a sole trader or to a partnership. These obligations fall into five broad groups:

(a) Much of company administration is subject to statute (CA 2006) and there are rules relating to directors and the company secretary (ss 154–259 & ss 270–280 CA 2006 respectively, although a private company no longer requires a company secretary). The conduct of meetings of shareholders and directors is subject to statutory control (ss 281–361 CA 2006), although the impact of such rules is lessened by the passing of the CA 2006 in respect of small companies, reflecting the informal way in which most private companies are run.

(b) The power of the directors, who in smaller companies will almost certainly be majority shareholders, are limited, in that certain things cannot be done while others can be done only with the agreement of the shareholders. Many of these constraints on directorial power relate to the ability of the directors to benefit themselves. For example, certain transactions between a director and the company requires approval of the members (s 197 CA 2006 – loans to directors – and s 190 CA 2006 – 'substantial property transactions'). The power of the directors to raise capital by the allotment of shares is restricted (ss 549–551 CA 2006).

(c) The ability of the directors or shareholders to do as they wish with the shares of the company is restricted, so that, for instance, a company cannot buy its own shares, although there are exceptions (ss 658–659 CA 2006).

(d) The major statutory requirement which imposes a continuing burden relates to company accounts. The financial results of the company must be presented to the shareholders in a balance sheet and profit and loss account (s 396 CA 2006). The length and technicality of the accounting rules mean that company accounts must, in effect, be prepared by a qualified accountant and a company must have its accounts checked (audited) by a qualified accountant (s 475 CA 2006 – see s 485 CA 2006 (private companies) and s 489 CA 2006 (public companies)). All companies must send their accounts to the registrar of companies, where they are open to public inspection, although small and medium sized companies, as defined by the CA 2006, can elect to send an abridged version instead. The obligation of a company to produce audited accounts in compliance with the CA 2006 imposes an annual financial burden on a company, although, 'small companies' (defined in s 477 CA 2006) have been exempted from the statutory audit unless members holding at least 10% by value of a class of shares require the company to obtain an audit. However, there can be little doubt that a number of business people think that the bureaucratic drawbacks are more than outweighed by the benefits of incorporation.

NOTE

One of the stated aims behind the CA 2006 was for the administrative burden involved in running a company, particularly, a private company, to be eased. This is reflected in some of the changes introduced by the CA 2006 in respect of the matters contained in the text, for example, the lessening of the strictness of personal liability in what was s 349 CA 1985, reductions of capital no longer requiring court approval and the need not to hold meetings. In addition, changes have been made to the directors' power to allot shares and the rules regulating certain contracts between a director and a company (known as the 'fair dealing' provisions under the CA 1985) have been tidied up and strengthened.